# Student Lecture Companion
## A Note-Taking Guide to Accompany

4<sup>th</sup> EDITION

# Programming and Problem Solving

with

C++

## Nell Dale
University of Texas at Austin

JONES AND BARTLETT PUBLISHERS
*Sudbury, Massachusetts*
BOSTON    TORONTO    LONDON    SINGAPORE

**World Headquarters**
Jones and Bartlett Publishers
40 Tall Pine Drive
Sudbury, MA 01776
978-443-5000
info@jbpub.com
www.jbpub.com

Jones and Bartlett Publishers Canada
2406 Nikanna Road
Mississauga, ON L5C 2W6
CANADA

Jones and Bartlett Publishers International
Barb House, Barb Mews
London W6 7PA
UK

Copyright 2005 by Jones and Bartlett Publishers, Inc.

ISBN: 0-7637-2691-5

Printed in the United States of America
08  07  06  05          10  9  8  7  6  5  4  3  2

# Contents

## How This Book Can Help You Learn

All of us have different learning styles. Some of us are visual learners, some more auditory, some learn better by doing an activity. Some students prefer to learn new material using visual aids. Some learn material better when they hear it in a lecture; others learn it better by reading it. Cognitive research has shown that no matter what your learning style, you will learn more if you are actively engaged in the learning process.

The Student Lecture Companion will help you learn by providing a structure to your notes and letting you utilize all of the learning styles mentioned above. Students don't need to copy down every word their professor says or recopy their entire Computer Science textbook. Do the assigned reading, listen in lecture, follow the key points your instructor is making, and write down meaningful notes. After reading and lectures, review your notes and pull out the most important points.

The Student Lecture Companion is your partner and guide in note-taking. Your Companion provides you with a visual guide that follows the chapter topics presented in your textbook, *Programming and Problem Solving with C++,* 4th Edition. If your instructor is using the PowerPoint slides that accompany the text, this guide will save you from having to write down everything that is on the slides. There is space provided for you to jot down the terms and concepts that you feel are most important to each lecture. By working with your Companion, you are seeing, hearing, writing, and, later, reading and reviewing. The more times you are exposed to the material, the better you will learn and understand it. Using different methods of exposure significantly increases your comprehension.

Your Companion is the perfect place to write down questions that you want to ask your professor later, interesting ideas that you want to discuss with your study group, or reminders to yourself to go back and study a certain concept again to make sure that you really got it.

Having organized notes is essential at exam time, when doing homework assignments, or when work-ing on programming problems. Your ability to easily locate the important concepts of a recent lecture will help you move along more rapidly, as you don't have to spend time rereading an entire chapter just to reinforce one point that you may not have quite understood.

Your Companion is a valuable resource. You've found a wonderful study partner!

## Note-Taking Tips

1.  It is easier to take notes if you are not hearing the information for the first time. Read the chapter or the material that is about to be discussed before class. This will help you to anticipate what will be said in class, and have an idea of what to write down. It will also help to read over your notes from the last class. This way you can avoid having to spend the first few minutes of class trying to remember where you left off last time.

2.  Don't waste your time trying to write down everything that your professor says. Instead, listen closely and only write down the important points. Review these important points after class to help remind you of related points that were made during the lecture.

3.  If the class discussion takes a spontaneous turn, pay attention and participate in the discussion. Only take notes on the conclusions that are relevant to the lecture.

4.  Emphasize main points in your notes. You may want to use a highlighter, special notation (asterisks, exclamation points), format (circle, underline), or placement on the page (indented, bulleted). You will find that when you try to recall these points, you will be able to actually picture them on the page.

5.  Be sure to copy down word-for-word specific formulas, laws, and theories.

6.  Hearing something repeated, stressed, or summed up can be a signal that it is an important concept to understand.

7.  Organize handouts, study guides, and exams in your notebook along with your lecture notes. It may be helpful to use a three-ring binder, so that you can insert pages wherever you need to.

8.  When taking notes, you might find it helpful to leave a wide margin on all four sides of the page. Doing this allows you to note names, dates, definitions, etc. for easy access and studying later. It may also be helpful to make notes of questions you want to ask your professor about or research later, ideas or relationships that you want explore more on your own, or concepts that you don't fully understand.

9.  It is best to maintain a separate notebook for each class. Labeling and dating your notes can be helpful when you need to look up information from previous lectures.

10. Make your notes legible, and take notes directly in your notebook. Chances are you won't recopy them no matter how noble your intentions. Spend the time you would have spent recopying the notes studying them instead, drawing conclusions and making connections that you didn't have time for in class.

11. Look over your notes after class while the lecture is still fresh in your mind. Fix illegible items and clarify anything you don't understand. Do this again right before the next class.

# Key Terms

**Abstract data type**  A data type whose properties (domain and operations) are specified independently of any particular implementation.

**Abstract step**  A step for which some implementation details remain unspecified.

**Abstraction barrier**  The invisible wall around a class object that encapsulates implementation details. The wall can be breached only through the public interface.

**Aggregate operation**  An operation on a data structure as a whole, as opposed to an operation on an individual component of the data structure.

**Algorithm**  A stepbystep procedure for solving a problem in a finite amount of time.

**Anonymous type**  A type that does not have an associated type identifier.

**Argument**  A variable or expression listed in a call to a function; also called actual argument or actual parameter.

**Argument list**  A mechanism by which functions communicate with each other.

**Arithmetic/logic unit (ALU)**  The component of the central processing unit that performs arithmetic and logical operations.

**Array**  A collection of components, all of the same type, ordered on N dimensions (N ? 1). Each component is accessed by N indexes, each of which represents the component's position within that dimension.

**Assembler**  A program that translates an assembly language program into machine code.

**Assembly language**  A lowlevel programming language in which a mnemonic is used to represent each of the machine language instructions for a particular computer.

**Assignment expression**  A C++ expression with (1) a value and (2) the side effect of storing the expression value into a memory location.

**Assignment statement**  A statement that stores the value of an expression into a variable.

**Automatic variable**  A variable for which memory is allocated and deallocated when control enters and exits the block in which it is declared.

**Auxiliary storage device**  A device that stores data in encoded form outside the computer's main memory.

**Base address**  The memory address of the first element of an array.

**Base class (superclass)**  The class being inherited from.

**Binary operator**  An operator that has two operands.

**Black box**  An electrical or mechanical device whose inner workings are hidden from view.

**C string**  In C and C++, a null-terminated sequence of characters stored in a char array.

**Central processing unit (CPU)**  The part of the computer that executes the instructions (program) stored in memory; made up of the arithmetic/logic unit and the control unit.

**Class**  A structured type in a programming language that is used to represent an abstract data type.

**Class member**  A component of a class. Class members may be either data or functions.

**Class object** (class instance)  A variable of a class type.

**Client**  Software that declares and manipulates objects of a particular class.

**Communication complexity**  A measure of the quantity of data passing through a module's interface.

**Compiler**  A program that translates a highlevel language into machine code.

**Complexity**  A measure of the effort expended by the computer in performing a computation, relative to the size of the computation.

**Composition (containment)**  A mechanism by which the internal data (the state) of one class includes an object of another class.

**Computer**  A programmable device that can store, retrieve, and process data.

**Computer program**  A sequence of instructions to be performed by a computer.

**Computer programming**  The process of planning a sequence of steps for a computer to follow.

**Concrete step**  A step for which the implementation details are fully specified.

**Constructor**  An operation that creates a new instance (variable) of an ADT.

**Control abstraction**  The separation of the logical properties of an action from its implementation.

**Control structure**  A statement used to alter the normally sequential flow of control.

**Control unit**  The component of the central processing unit that controls the actions of the other components so that instructions (the program) are executed in the correct sequence.

**Countcontrolled loop**  A loop that executes a specified number of times.

**Data**  Information in a form a computer can use.

**Data abstraction**  The separation of a data type's logical properties from its implementation.

**Data flow**  The flow of information from the calling code to a function and from the function back to the calling code.

**Data representation**  The concrete form of data used to represent the abstract values of an abstract data type.

**Data type**  A specific set of data values, along with a set of operations on those values.

**Declaration**  A statement that associates an identifier with a data object, a function, or a data type so that the programmer can refer to that item by name.

**Demotion (narrowing)**  The conversion of a value from a "higher" type to a "lower" type according to a programming language's precedence of data types. Demotion may cause loss of information.

**Derived class (subclass)**  The class that inherits.

**Documentation**  The written text and comments that make a program easier for others to understand, use, and modify.

**Driver**  A simple main function that is used to call a function being tested. The use of a driver permits direct control of the testing process.

**Dynamic binding**  The run-time determination of which function to call for a particular object.

**Editor**  An interactive program used to create and modify source programs or data.

**Encapsulation**  Hiding a module implementation in a separate block with a formally specified interface.

**Enumeration type**  A user-defined data type whose domain is an ordered set of literal values expressed as identifiers.

**Enumerator**  One of the values in the domain of an enumeration type.

**Evaluate**  To compute a new value by performing a specified set of operations on given values.

**Event counter**  A variable that is incremented each time a particular event occurs.

**Eventcontrolled loop**  A loop that terminates when something happens inside the loop body to signal that the loop should be exited.

**Expression**  An arrangement of identifiers, literals, and operators that can be evaluated to compute a value of a given type.

**Expression statement**  A statement formed by appending a semicolon to an expression.

**External representation**  The printable (character) form of a data value.

**Field (member, in C++)**  A component of a record.

**File**  A named area in secondary storage that is used to hold a collection of data; the collection of data itself.

**Flow of control**  The order in which the computer executes statements in a program.

**Function**  A subprogram in C++.

**Function call (function invocation)**  The mechanism that transfers control to a function.

**Function call (to a void function)**  A statement that transfers control to a void function. In C++, this statement is the name of the function, followed by a list of arguments.

**Function definition**  A function declaration that includes the body of the function.

**Function prototype**  A function declaration without the body of the function.

**Function value type**  The data type of the result value returned by a function.

**Functional cohesion**  A property of a module in which all concrete steps are directed toward solving just one problem, and any significant subproblems are written as abstract steps.

**Functional cohesion**  The principle that a module should perform exactly one abstract action.

**Functional decomposition**  A technique for developing software in which the problem is divided into more easily handled subproblems, the solutions of which create a solution to the overall problem.

**Functional equivalence**  A property of a module that performs exactly the same operation as the abstract step it defines. A pair of modules are also functionally equivalent to each other when they perform exactly the same operation.

**Hardware**  The physical components of a computer.

**Hierarchical record**  A record in which at least one of the components is itself a record.

**Identifier**  A name associated with a function or data object and used to refer to that function or data object.

**Information**  Any knowledge that can be communicated.

**Information hiding**  The encapsulation and hiding of implementation details to keep the user of an abstraction from depending on or incorrectly manipulating these details.

**Inheritance**  A mechanism by which one class acquires the properties-the data and operations-of another class.

**Input/output (I/O) devices**  The parts of the computer that accept data to be processed (input) and present the results of that processing (output).

**Interactive system**  A system that allows direct communication between user and computer.

**Interface**  A connecting link at a shared boundary that allows independent systems to meet and act on or communicate with each other.

**Interface**  A connecting link at a shared boundary that permits independent systems to meet and act on or communicate with each other. Also, the formal description of the purpose of a subprogram and the mechanism for communicating with it.

**Internal representation**  The form in which a data value is stored inside the memory unit.

**Iteration**  An individual pass through, or repetition of, the body of a loop.

**Iteration counter**  A counter variable that is incremented with each iteration of a loop.

**Iterator**  An operation that allows us to process-one at a time-all the components in an instance of an ADT.

**Length**  The number of values currently stored in a list.

**Lifetime**  The period of time during program execution when an identifier has memory allocated to it.

**List**  A variable-length, linear collection of homogeneous components.

**Literal value**  Any constant value written in a program.

**Local variable**  A variable declared within a block and not accessible outside of that block.

**Loop**  A control structure that causes a statement or group of statements to be executed repeatedly.

**Loop entry**  The point at which the flow of control reaches the first statement inside a loop.

**Loop exit**  The point at which the repetition of the loop body ends and control passes to the first statement following the loop.

**Loop test**  The point at which the While expression is evaluated and the decision is made either to begin a new iteration or skip to the statement immediately following the loop.

**Machine language**  The language, made up of binarycoded instructions, that is used directly by the computer.

**Member selector**  The expression used to access components of a struct variable. It is formed by using the struct variable name and the member name, separated by a dot (period).

**Memory unit**  Internal data storage in a computer.

**Metalanguage**  A language that is used to write the syntax rules for another language.

**Mixed type expression**  An expression that contains operands of different data types; also called mixed mode expression.

**Module**  A selfcontained collection of steps that solves a problem or subproblem; can contain both concrete and abstract steps.

**Name precedence**  The precedence that a local identifier in a function has over a global identifier with the same name in any references that the function makes to that identifier; also called name hiding.

**Named constant (symbolic constant)**  A location in memory, referenced by an identifier, that contains a data value that cannot be changed.

**Named type**  A user-defined type whose declaration includes a type identifier that gives a name to the type.

**Nonlocal identifier** With respect to a given block, any identifier declared outside that block.

**Object program** The machine language version of a source program.

**Object-oriented design** A technique for developing software in which the solution is expressed in terms of objects-self-contained entities composed of data and operations on that data.

**Object-oriented programming (OOP)** The use of data abstraction, inheritance, and dynamic binding to construct programs that are collections of interacting objects.

**Observer** An operation that allows us to observe the state of an instance of an ADT without changing it.

**Onedimensional array** A structured collection of components, all of the same type, that is given a single name. Each component (array element) is accessed by an index that indicates the component's position within the collection.

**Operating system** A set of programs that manages all of the computer's resources.

**Out-of-bounds array index** An index value that, in C++, is either less than 0 or greater than the array size minus 1.

**Parameter** A variable declared in a function heading; also called formal argument or formal parameter.

**Peripheral device** An input, output, or auxiliary storage device attached to a computer.

**Polymorphic operation** An operation that has multiple meanings depending on the type of the object to which it is bound at run time.

**Postcondition** An assertion that should be true after a module has executed.

**Precision** The maximum number of significant digits.

**Precondition** An assertion that must be true before a module begins executing.

**Programming** Planning or scheduling the performance of a task or an event.

**Programming language** A set of rules, symbols, and special words used to construct a computer program.

**Promotion (widening)** The conversion of a value from a "lower" type to a "higher" type according to a programming language's precedence of data types.

**Range of values** The interval within which values of a numeric type must fall, specified in terms of the largest and smallest allowable values.

**Record (structure, in C++)** A structured data type with a fixed number of components that are accessed by name. The components may be heterogeneous (of different types).

**Reference parameter** A parameter that receives the location (memory address) of the caller's argument.

**Representational error** Arithmetic error that occurs when the precision of the true result of an arithmetic operation is greater than the precision of the machine.

**Reserved word** A word that has special meaning in C++; it cannot be used as a programmer-defined identifier.

**Scope** The region of program code where it is legal to reference (use) an identifier.

**Scope rules** The rules that determine where in the program an identifier may be accessed, given the point where that identifier is declared.

**Selfdocumenting code** Program code containing meaningful identifiers as well as judiciously used clarifying comments.

**Semantics** The set of rules that determines the meaning of instructions written in a programming language.

**Short-circuit (conditional) evaluation**  Evaluation of a logical expression in left-to-right order with evaluation stopping as soon as the final truth value can be determined.

**Side effect**  Any effect of one function on another that is not a part of the explicitly defined interface between them.

**Significant digits**  Those digits from the first nonzero digit on the left to the last nonzero digit on the right (plus any 0 digits that are exact).

**Simple (atomic) data type**  A data type in which each value is atomic (indivisible).

**Software**  Computer programs; the set of all programs available on a computer.

**Software engineering**  The application of traditional engineering methodologies and techniques to the development of software.

**Software piracy**  The unauthorized copying of software for either personal use or use by others.

**Sorting**  Arranging the components of a list into order (for instance, words into alphabetical order or numbers into ascending or descending order).

**Source program**  A program written in a highlevel programming language.

**Static binding**  The compile-time determination of which function to call for a particular object.

**Static variable**  A variable for which memory remains allocated throughout the execution of the entire program.

**Structured (procedural) programming**  The construction of programs that are collections of interacting functions or procedures.

**Structured data type**  A data type in which each value is a collection of components and whose organization is characterized by the method used to access individual components. The allowable operations on a structured data type include the storage and retrieval of individual components.

**Stub**  A dummy function that assists in testing part of a program. A stub has the same name and interface as a function that actually would be called by the part of the program being tested, but it is usually much simpler.

**Switch expression**  The expression whose value determines which switch label is selected. It cannot be a floating-point or string expression.

**Syntax**  The formal rules governing how valid instructions are written in a programming language.

**Termination condition**  The condition that causes a loop to be exited.

**Test plan**  A document that specifies how a program is to be tested.

**Test plan implementation**  Using the test cases specified in a test plan to verify that a program outputs the predicted results.

**Testing the state of a stream**  The act of using a C++ stream object in a logical expression as if it were a Boolean variable; the result is true if the last I/O operation on that stream succeeded, and false otherwise.

**Transformer**  An operation that builds a new value of the ADT, given one or more previous values of the type.

**Twodimensional array**  A collection of components, all of the same type, structured in two dimensions. Each component is accessed by a pair of indexes that represent the component's position in each dimension.

**Type casting**  The explicit conversion of a value from one data type to another; also called type conversion.

**Type coercion**  The implicit (automatic) conversion of a value from one data type to another.

**Unary operator**  An operator that has just one operand.

**Value parameter**  A parameter that receives a copy of the value of the corresponding argument.

**Value-returning function**  A function that returns a single value to its caller and is invoked from within an expression.

**Variable**  A location in memory, referenced by an identifier, that contains a data value that can be changed.

**Virus**  A computer program that replicates itself, often with the goal of spreading to other computers without authorization, and possibly with the intent of doing harm.

**Void function (procedure)**  A function that does not return a function value to its caller and is invoked as a separate statement.

# Chapter 1: Overview of Programming and Problem Solving

**Notes**

### Chapter 1 Topics

- Computer Programming
- Programming Life-Cycle Phases
- Creating an Algorithm
- Machine Language vs. High Level Languages
- Compilation and Execution Processes
- C++ History
- Computer Components
- Computing Profession Ethics
- Problem-Solving Techniques

### What is Computer Programming?

- It is the process of planning a sequence of steps(called instructions) for a computer to follow.

> STEP 1
>
> STEP 2
>
> STEP 3

. . .

## Programming Life Cycle Phases

- Problem-Solving
- Implementation
- Maintenance

4

## Problem-Solving Phase

- Analyze the problem and specify what the solution must do

- Develop a general solution(algorithm) to solve the problem

- Verify that your solution really solves the problem

5

## Sample Problem

Suppose a programmer needs to determine an employee's weekly wages.

*How would the calculations be done by hand?*

6

## One Employee's Wages

In one week an employee works 52 hours at the hourly pay rate of $24.75. Assume a 40.0 hour normal work week and an overtime pay rate factor of 1.5.

*What are the employee's wages?*

```
40 x $ 24.75          =   $990.00
12 x 1.5 x $ 24.75=   $445.50
                          _____
                      $   1435.50
```

7

## Weekly Wages, in General

If hours are more than 40.0
    wages =
        (40.0 * payRate) +
        (hours - 40.0) * 1.5 *payRate

---

**RECALL EXAMPLE**

(40  x  $ 24.75) +(12 x 1.5 x $ 24.75) = $1435.50

---

otherwise
    wages = hours * payRate

8

## An Algorithm

- An algorithm is a step-by-step procedure for solving a problem
  - with a finite amount of data
  - in a finite amount of time

9

**Notes**

### Algorithm to Determine an Employee's Weekly Wages

1. Get the employee's hourly payRate
2. Get the hours worked this week
3. Calculate this week's regular wages
4. Calculate this week's overtime wages(if any)
5. Add the regular wages to overtime wages(if any) to determine total wages for the week

10

### What is a Programming Language?

- A programming language is a language with strict grammar rules, symbols, and special words used to construct a computer program

11

### Implementation Phase: Program

- Translating your algorithm into a programming language is called coding
- With C++, you use

Documentation -- your written comments

Compiler -- translates your program into machine language

Main Program -- may call subalgorithms

12

### Implementation Phase: Test

- Testing your program means running(executing) your program on the computer, to see if it produces correct results

- If it does not, then you must find out what is wrong with your program or algorithm and fix it--this is called debugging

13

### Maintenance Phase

- Use and modify the program to meet changing requirements or correct errors that show up in using it
- Maintenance begins when your program is put into use and accounts for the majority of effort on most programs

14

### Programming Life Cycle

1 Problem-Solving Phase
   Analysis and Specification
   General Solution(Algorithm)
   Verify

2 Implementation Phase
   Concrete Solution(Program)
   Test

3 Maintenance Phase
   Use
   Maintain

15

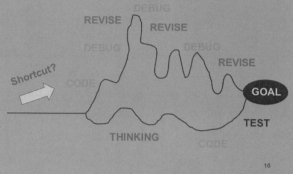

## A Tempting Shortcut?

## Memory Organization

- Two circuit states correspond to 0 and 1
- Bit(short for binary digit) refers to a single 0 or 1
- Bit patterns represent both the computer instructions and computer data
- 1 byte = 8 bits
- 1 KB = 1024 bytes
- 1 MB = 1024 x 1024 = 1,048,576 bytes

17

## How Many Possible Digits?

- Binary (base 2) numbers use 2 digits: just 0 and 1

- Decimal(base 10) numbers use 10 digits: 0 through 9

18

## Machine Language

- Is not portable

- Runs only on a specific type of computer

- Is made up of binary-coded instructions(strings of 0s and 1s)

- Is the language that can be directly used by the computer

19

## High Level Languages

- Are portable

- User writes program in language similar to natural language

- Examples -- FORTRAN, COBOL, Pascal, Ada, Modula-2, C++, Java

- Most are standardized by ISO/ANSI to provide an official description of the language

20

## Three C++ Program Stages

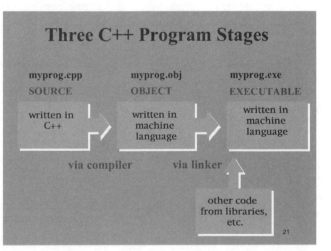

## Java Programming Language

- Achieves portability by using both a compiler and an interpreter

- First, a Java compiler translates a Java program into an intermediate Bytecode--not machine language

- Then, an interpreter program called the Java Virtual Machine(JVM) translates a single instruction in the bytecode program to machine language and immediately runs it, one at a time

22

## Basic Control Structures

- A sequence is a series of statements that execute one after another

- A selection(branch) statement is used to determine which of two different statements to execute depending on certain conditions

- A looping(repetition) statement is used to repeat statements while certain conditions are met

- A subprogram is a smaller part of another program; a collection of subprograms solves the original problem

23

## SEQUENCE

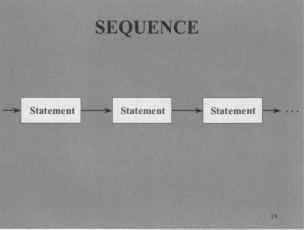

24

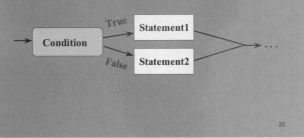

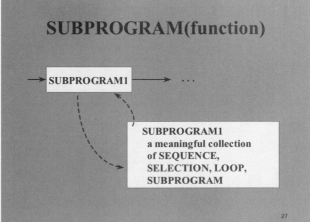

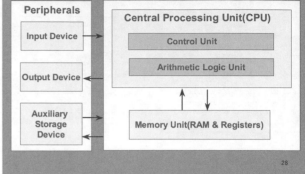

## Computer Components

**Peripherals**

| Input Device |

| Output Device |

| Auxiliary Storage Device |

**Central Processing Unit(CPU)**

| Control Unit |

| Arithmetic Logic Unit |

| Memory Unit(RAM & Registers) |

28

## Memory Unit

- Is an ordered sequence of storage cells, each capable of holding a piece of information

- Each cell has its own unique address

- The information held can be input data, computed values, or your program instructions

29

## Central Processing Unit

- Has two components to execute program instructions

  - Arithmetic/Logic Unit performs arithmetic operations, and makes logical comparisons

  - Control Unit controls the order in which your program instructions are executed

30

**Notes**

_____
_____
_____
_____
_____
_____
_____
_____
_____
_____
_____
_____
_____
_____
_____
_____
_____
_____
_____
_____
_____
_____
_____
_____
_____
_____
_____
_____
_____
_____
_____
_____
_____
_____

## Peripherals

- Are input, output, or auxiliary storage devices attached to a computer

  - Input Devices include keyboard and mouse

  - Output Devices include printers, video display, LCD screens

  - Auxiliary Storage Devices include disk drives, scanners, CD-ROM and DVD-ROM drives, modems, sound cards, speakers, and digital cameras

31

## Some C++ History

- 1972 : Dennis Ritchie at Bell Labs designs C and 90% of UNIX is then written in C

- Late 70's : OOP becomes popular

- Bjarne Stroustrup at Bell Labs adds features to C to form "C with Classes"

- 1983 : Name  C++  first used

- 1998 : ISO/ANSI standardization of C++

32

## Computing Profession Ethics

- Copy software only with permission from the copyright holder

- Give credit to another programmer by name whenever using his/her code

- Use computer resources only with permission

- Guard the privacy of confidential data

- Use software engineering principles to develop software free from errors

33

### What are the Areas of Computer Science?
The Computing Curriculum 1991(ACM/IEEE)

- Algorithms and Data Structures
- Architecture
- Artificial Intelligence and Robotics
- Database and Information Retrieval
- Human-Computer Communication
- Numerical and Symbolic Computation
- Operating Systems
- Programming Languages
- Software Engineering
- Social and Professional Context

34

## Problem Solving Techniques

- **Ask questions -- about the data, the process, the output, error conditions**

- **Look for familiar things -- certain situations arise again and again**

- **Solve by analogy -- it may give you a place to start**

- **Use means-ends analysis -- determine the I/O and then work out the details**

35

## More Problem Solving Techniques

- **Divide and conquer -- break up large problems into manageable units**

- **Building-block approach -- can you solve small pieces of the problem?**

- **Merge solutions -- instead of joining them end to end to avoid duplicate steps**

- **Overcome mental block -- by rewriting the problem in your own words**

36

## Is a year a leap year?

**Problem** You need to write a set of instructions that can be used to determine whether a year is a leap year. The instructions must be very clear because they are to be used by a class of fourth graders, who have just learned about multiplication and division. They plan to use the instructions as part of an assignment to determine whether any of their relatives were born in a leap year.

37

## Leap Year Algorithm

Prompt the user to enter a four-digit year
Read the year
If IsLeapYear
    Write "Year is a leap year"
Otherwise
    Write "Year is not a leap year"

38

## IsLeapYear Algorithm

Divide the year by 4
If the remainder isn't zero,
    Return false(The year is not a leap year)
Otherwise divide the year by 10 and
If the remainder isn't 0,
    Return true(The year is a leap year)
    Otherwise, divide the year by 400 and
    If the remainder isn't 0
        Return false(The year is not a leap year)
        Otherwise, Return true(The year is a leap year)

39

**Notes**

## C++ Program

```
//********************************************************
// LeapYear program
// This program inputs a year and prints whether the year
// is a leap year or not
//********************************************************
#include <iostream>        // Access output stream

using namespace std;       // Access cout, endl, cin

bool IsLeapYear(int);      // Prototype for subalgorithm


int main()
{
  …
}
```
40

## Body of Main

```
{
    int year;              // Year to be tested
    cout << "Enter a year AD, for example, 1997."
         << endl;          // Prompt for input
    cin >> year;           // Read year

    if(IsLeapYear(year))          // Test for leap year
        cout << year << " is a leap year."  << endl;
    else
        cout << year << " is not a leap year."  << endl;
    return 0;              // Indicates successful
                          //   completion

}
```
41

## IsLeapYear

```
bool IsLeapYear(int year)
// IsLeapYear returns true if year is a leap year and
// false otherwise
{
    if(year % 4 != 0)        // Is year not divisible by 4?
        return false;        // If so, can't be a leap year
    else if(year % 100 != 0) // Is year not a multiple of 100?
        return true;         // If so, is a leap year
    else if(year % 400 != 0) // Is year not a multiple of 400?
        return false;        // If so, then is not a leap year
    else
        return true;         // Is a leap year
}
```
42

## Notes

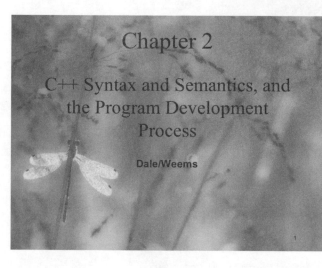

**Chapter 2**

C++ Syntax and Semantics, and the Program Development Process

Dale/Weems

**Chapter 2 Topics**

- Programs Composed of Several Functions
- Syntax Templates
- Legal C++ Identifiers
- Assigning Values to Variables
- Declaring Named Constants
- String Concatenation
- Output Statements
- C++ Program Comments

**A C++ program is a collection of one or more functions**

- There must be a function called main()

- Execution always begins with the first statement in function main()

- Any other functions in your program are subprograms and are not executed until they are called

**Notes**

## Program With Several Functions

```
┌ ─ ─ ─ ─ ─ ─ ─ ─ ─ ─ ─ ─ ─ ─ ┐
│    ┌─────────────────────┐    │
│    │    main  function   │    │
│    └─────────────────────┘    │
│    ┌─────────────────────┐    │
│    │   square  function  │    │
│    └─────────────────────┘    │
│    ┌─────────────────────┐    │
│    │    cube  function   │    │
└ ─ ─└─────────────────────┘─ ─ ┘
```

4

## Program With Three Functions

```
#include <iostream>

int Square(int);        // Declares these two
int Cube(int);          // value-returning functions

using namespace std;

int main()
{
    cout << "The square of 27 is "
        << Square(27)<< endl;    // Function call

    cout << "The cube of 27 is "
        << Cube(27)<< endl;      // Function call
    return 0;
}
```

5

## Rest of Program

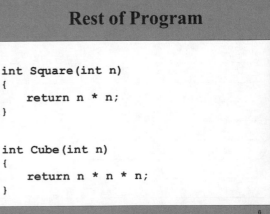

```
int Square(int n)
{
    return n * n;
}


int Cube(int n)
{
    return n * n * n;
}
```

6

## Output of program

The square of 27 is 729
The cube of 27 is 19683

7

## Shortest C++ Program

type of returned value          name of function

```
int  main()
{

     return 0;

}
```

8

## *What is in a heading?*

type of returned value          name of function          says no parameters

```
int  main(     )
```

9

## Block(Compound Statement)

- A **block** is a sequence of zero or more statements enclosed by a pair of curly braces { }

SYNTAX

```
{
        Statement (optional)
        .
        .
        .
}
```

10

## Every C++ function has 2 parts

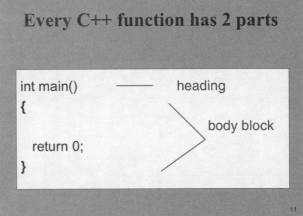

```
int main()  ────  heading
{

    return 0;
}
```
body block

11

## *What is an Identifier?*

An **identifier** is the name used for a data object(a variable or a constant), or for a function, in a C++ program

Beware: C++ is a case-sensitive language

Using **meaningful identifiers** is a good programming practice

12

## Identifiers

- An *identifier* must start with a letter or underscore, and be followed by zero or more letters
  (A-Z, a-z), digits(0-9), or underscores
- VALID

  age_of_dog         taxRateY2K
  PrintHeading        ageOfHorse
- NOT VALID *(Why?)*

  age#       2000TaxRate      Age-Of-Cat

13

## More About Identifiers

- Some C++ compilers recognize only the first 32 characters of an identifier as significant
- Then these identifiers are considered the same:

  age_Of_This_Old_Rhinoceros_At_My_Zoo
  age_Of_This_Old_Rhinoceros_At_My_Safari
- Consider these:

  Age_Of_This_Old_Rhinoceros_At_My_Zoo
  age_Of_This_Old_Rhinoceros_At_My_Zoo

14

## C++ Data Types

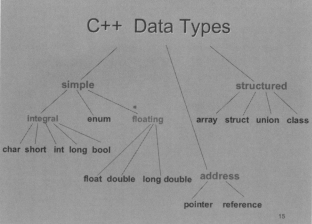

15

**Notes**

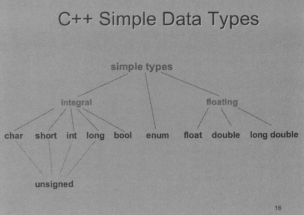

### C++ Simple Data Types

```
                    simple types
                   /            \
           integral              floating
          / | | | \  \          /    |     \
  char short int long bool enum float double long double
            \  |  /
           unsigned
```

16

---

## Standard Data Types in C++

● **Integral Types**
  ■ represent whole numbers and their negatives
  ■ declared as int, short, or long

● **Floating Types**
  ■ represent real numbers with a decimal point
  ■ declared as float, or double

● **Character Types**
  ■ represent single characters
  ■ declared as char

17

---

## Samples of C++ Data Values

int  sample values
   4578          -4578              0

float  sample values
   95.274         95.             .265

char  sample values
   'B'     'd'     '4'     '?'     '*'

18

### What is a Variable?

● A variable is a location in memory that can be referred to by an identifier and in which a data value that can be changed is stored

● Declaring a variable means specifying both its name and its data type

19

### What Does a Variable Declaration Do?

```
int    ageOfDog;
float  taxRate;
char   middleInitial;
```

A declaration tells the compiler to allocate enough memory to hold a value of this data type and to associate the identifier with this location

4 bytes for taxRateY2K          1 byte for middleInitial

20

### C++ Data Type String

● A string is a sequence of characters enclosed in double quotes

● Sample string values
"Hello"    "Year 2000"    "1234"

● The empty string(null string)contains no characters and is written as    ""

21

**Notes**

## More About Type String

- A string is not a built-in(standard)type
  - It is a programmer-defined data type
  - It is provided in the C++ standard library

- String operations include
  - Comparing 2 string values
  - Searching a string for a particular character
  - Joining one string to another

22

## *What is a Named Constant?*

- A named constant is a location in memory that can be referred to by an identifier and in which a data value that cannot be changed is stored

Valid constant declarations

```
const  string  STARS = "****";
const  float   NORMAL_TEMP = 98.6;
const  char    BLANK = ' ';
const  int     VOTING_AGE = 18;
const  float   MAX_HOURS = 40.0;
```

23

## Giving a Value to a Variable

Assign(give)a value to a variable by using the assignment operator =

Variable declarations

```
string   firstName;
char     middleInitial;
char     letter;
int      ageOfDog;
```

Valid assignment statements

```
firstName = "Fido";
middleInitial = 'X';
letter = middleInitial;
ageOfDog = 12;
```

24

*What is an Expression in C++?*

● An expression is a valid arrangement of variables, constants, and operators

● In C++ each expression can be evaluated to compute a value of a given type

● The value of the expression
9 + 5  is  14

25

Assignment Operator Syntax

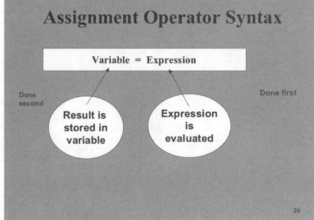

Variable = Expression

Done second

Done first

Result is stored in variable

Expression is evaluated

26

String Concatenation(+)

● Concatenation is a binary operation that uses the + operator

● At least one of the operands must be a string variable or named string constant-- the other operand can be a string literal or a char variable, literal, or constant

27

## Concatenation Example

```
const    string WHEN = "Tomorrow";
const    char  EXCLAMATION = '!';
string   message1;
string   message2;

message1 = "Yesterday ";
message2 = "and ";
message1 = message1 + message2 +
              WHEN + EXCLAMATION;
```

28

## Insertion Operator(<<)

- Variable cout is predefined to denote an output stream that goes to the standard output device(display screen)

- The insertion operator << called "put to" takes 2 operands

- The left operand is a stream expression, such as cout

- The right operand is an expression of a simple type or a string constant

29

## Output Statements

SYNTAX

```
cout << Expression  << Expression ...;
```

These examples yield the same output:

```
cout << "The answer is ";
cout << 3 * 4;
```

```
cout << "The answer is " << 3 * 4;
```

30

## *Is compilation the first step?*

- No; before your source program is compiled, it is first examined by the preprocessor that
  - removes all comments from source code
  - handles all preprocessor directives--they begin with the # character such as
    #include <iostream>
  - This include tells the preprocessor to look in the standard include directory for the header file called iostream and insert its contents into your source code

31

## No I/O is built into C++

- Instead, a library provides an output stream

32

## Using Libraries

- A library has 2 parts
  Interface(stored in a header file)tells what items are in the library and how to use them
  Implementation(stored in another file)contains the definitions of the items in the library

- #include <iostream>
  Refers to the header file for the *iostream* library needed for use of cout and endl.

33

## Function Concept in Math

Function definition

$$f(x) = 5x - 3$$

Parameter of function

Name of function

When x = 1, f(x)= 2 is the returned value

When x = 4, f(x)= 17 is the returned value

Returned value is determined by the function definition and by the values of any parameters

34

## C++ Program

```
// *******************************************************
//  PrintName program
//  This program prints a name in two different formats
// *******************************************************

#include <iostream>          // for cout and endl
#include <string>            // for data type string

using namespace std;

const  string  FIRST = "Herman";   // Person's first name
const  string  LAST = "Smith";     // Person's last name
const  char    MIDDLE = 'G';       // Person's middle initial
```

35

## C++ Code Continued

```
int  main()
{
    string    firstLast;    // Name in first-last format
    string    lastFirst;    // Name in last-first format


    firstLast = FIRST + " " + LAST;
    cout  << "Name in first-last format is "  << endl
          << firstLast  << endl;

    lastFirst = LAST + ", " + FIRST + ' ';
    cout  << "Name in first-last format is "  << endl
          << lastFirst  << MIDDLE  << '.'  << endl;

    return  0;
}
```

36

## Output of Program

Name in first-last format is
   Herman Smith
Name in last-first-initial format is
   Smith, Herman G.

37

## Creating a Chessboard

**Problem** Your college is hosting a chess tournament, and the people running the tournament want to record the final positions of the pieces in each game on a sheet of paper with a chessboard preprinted on it. Your job is to write a program to preprint these pieces of paper. The chessboard is an eight-by-eight pattern of squares that alternate between black and white, with the upper left square being white. You need to print out squares of light characters(spaces)and dark characters(such as *)in this pattern to form the chessboard.

38

## Chessboard

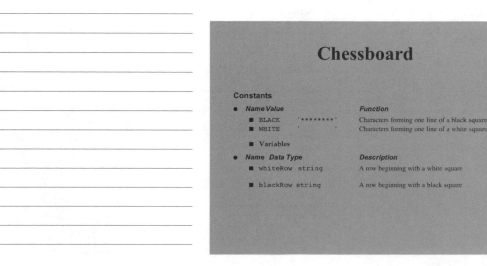

**Constants**

- *Name Value*          *Function*
  - BLACK   '********'     Characters forming one line of a black square
  - WHITE   '        '     Characters forming one line of a white square
  - Variables
- *Name  Data Type*      *Description*
  - whiteRow string      A row beginning with a white square
  - blackRow string      A row beginning with a black square

39

# Notes

## Algorithm

Repeat four times
   Output five whiteRows
   Output five blackRows

40

## C++ Program

```
//*********************************************************
// Chessboard program
// This program prints a chessboard pattern that is
// built up from basic strings of white and black
// characters.
//*********************************************************
#include <iostream>
#include <string>
using namespace std;
const string BLACK = "********"; // Define black square line
const string WHITE = "        "; // Define white square line
```

41

## C++ Program

```
int main()
{
    string whiteRow;    // White square beginning row
    string blackRow;    // Black square beginning row
    // Create a white-black row
    whiteRow = WHITE + BLACK + WHITE + BLACK +
               WHITE + BLACK + WHITE + BLACK;
    // Create a black-white row
    blackRow = BLACK + WHITE + BLACK + WHITE +
               BLACK + WHITE + BLACK + WHITE;
```

42

## C++ Program

```
    // Print five white-black rows
    cout << whiteRow << endl;
    cout << whiteRow << endl;
    cout << whiteRow << endl;
    cout << whiteRow << endl;
    cout << whiteRow << endl;

    // Print five black-white rows
    cout << blackRow << endl;
    cout << blackRow << endl;
    cout << blackRow << endl;
    cout << blackRow << endl;
    cout << blackRow << endl;
    // Print rest of the rows
    ...
    return 0;
}
```

43

**Notes**

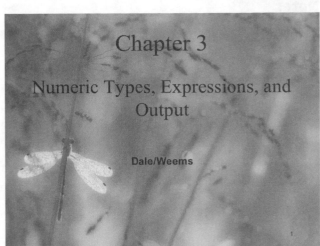

Chapter 3

Numeric Types, Expressions, and Output

Dale/Weems

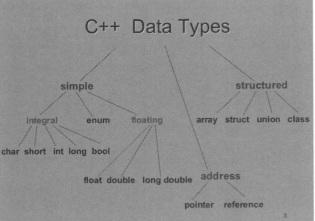

## Chapter 3 Topics

- Constants of Type int and float
- Evaluating Arithmetic Expressions
- Implicit Type Coercion and Explicit Type Conversion
- Calling a Value-Returning Function
- Using Function Arguments
- Using C++ Library Functions in Expressions
- Calling a Void Function
- C++ Manipulators to Format Output
- String Operations length,find,and substr

## C++ Data Types

simple

structured

integral    enum    floating

array  struct  union  class

char  short  int  long  bool

float  double  long double    address

pointer  reference

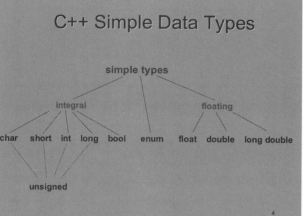

## C++ Simple Data Types

simple types

integral                    floating

char  short  int  long  bool  enum  float  double  long double

unsigned

4

## Standard Data Types in C++

● **Integral Types**
  ■ represent whole numbers and their negatives
  ■ declared as int, short, or long

● **Floating Types**
  ■ represent real numbers with a decimal point
  ■ declared as float or double

● **Character Type**
  ■ represents single characters
  ■ declared as char

5

## Samples of C++ Data Values

int sample values
  4578          -4578          0

float sample values
  95.274        95.              .265
  9521E-3       -95E-1          95.213E2

char sample values
  'B'    'd'      '4'    '?'      '*'

6

**Notes**

## Scientific Notation

$2.7E4$  means  $2.7 \times 10^4$  =

                          2.7000  =

                          27000.0

$2.7E-4$  means  $2.7 \times 10^{-4}$  =

                          0002.7  =

                          0.00027

7

## More About Floating Point Values

- Floating point numbers have an integer part and a fractional part, with a decimal point in between. Either the integer part or the fractional part, but not both, may be missing

Examples    18.4     500.    .8    -127.358

- Alternatively, floating point values can have an exponent, as in scientific notation--the number preceding the letter E doesn't need to include a decimal point

Examples    1.84E1    5E2    8E-1    -.127358E3

8

## Division Operator

- The result of the division operator depends on the type of its operands
- If one or both operands has a floating point type, the result is a floating point type. Otherwise, the result is an integer type

- Examples

    11 / 4      has value  2
    11.0 / 4.0  has value  2.75
    11 / 4.0    has value  2.75

9

## Main returns an int value to the operating system

```
//************************************************************
// FreezeBoil  program
// This program computes the midpoint between
// the freezing and boiling points of water
//************************************************************
#include  < iostream >
using  namespace  std;
const  float FREEZE_PT = 32.0;  // Freezing point of
water
const  float BOIL_PT =  212.0;  // Boiling point of water

int  main()
{
    float avgTemp;       // Holds the result of averaging
                         //   FREEZE_PT and BOIL_PT
```

10

## Function main Continued

```
    cout << "Water freezes at " << FREEZE_PT << endl;
    cout  << " and boils at " << BOIL_PT
         << " degrees."  << endl;

    avgTemp  =  FREEZE_PT  +  BOIL_PT;
    avgTemp  =  avgTemp  /  2.0;

    cout  << "Halfway between is ";
    cout  <<  avgTemp  <<  " degrees." <<  endl;

    return  0;
}
```

11

## Modulus Operator

- The modulus operator % can only be used with integer type operands and always has an integer type result
- Its result is the integer type remainder of an integer division
- Example

    11 % 4  has value  3 because

$$\begin{array}{r} R = ? \\ 4\overline{)\ 11} \end{array}$$

12

**Notes**

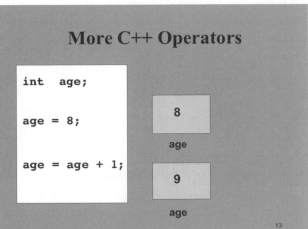

### More C++ Operators

```
int  age;

age = 8;

age = age + 1;
```

8
age

9
age

13

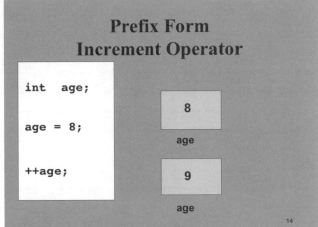

### Prefix Form
### Increment Operator

```
int  age;

age = 8;

++age;
```

8
age

9
age

14

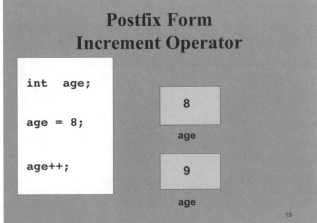

### Postfix Form
### Increment Operator

```
int  age;

age = 8;

age++;
```

8
age

9
age

15

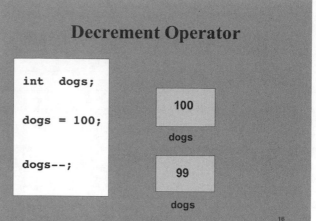

## Decrement Operator

```
int   dogs;

dogs = 100;

dogs--;
```

```
100
```
dogs

```
99
```
dogs

16

## Which Form to Use

● When the increment(or decrement) operator is used in a "*stand alone*" statement solely to add one(or subtract one) from a variable's value, it can be used in either prefix or postfix form

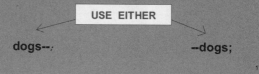

USE EITHER

dogs--;                          --dogs;

17

## BUT...

● When the increment(or decrement) operator is used in a statement with other operators, the prefix and postfix forms can yield *different* results

We'll see how later . . .

18

## What is an Expression in C++?

- An **expression** is a valid arrangement of variables, constants, and operators

- In C++ each expression can be evaluated to compute a value of a given type

- The value of the expression
  9.3 * 4.5   is   41.85

19

## Operators can be

| | | |
|---|---|---|
| binary | involving 2 operands | 2 + 3 |
| unary | involving 1 operand | - 3 |
| ternary | involving 3 operands | *later* |

20

## Some C++ Operators

| Precedence | Operator | Description |
|---|---|---|
| *Higher* | ( ) | Function call |
| | + | Positive |
| | - | Negative |
| | * | Multiplication |
| | / | Division |
| | % | Modulus (remainder) |
| | + | Addition |
| | - | Subtraction |
| *Lower* | = | Assignment |

21

## Precedence

- Higher Precedence determines which operator is applied first in an expression having several operators

22

## Associativity

- Left to right associativity means that in an expression having 2 operators with the same priority, the left operator is applied first

- In C++ the binary operators
  *, /, %, +, -  are all left associative

- Expression  9 - 5 - 1  means(9 - 5) - 1
                                                 4 - 1
                                                   3

23

## Evaluate the Expression

```
        7 * 10 - 5 % 3 * 4 + 9
       (7 * 10) - 5 % 3 * 4 + 9
          70 - 5 % 3 * 4 + 9
          70 -(5 % 3) * 4 + 9
           70 -  2  * 4 + 9
          70 -( 2 * 4) + 9
             70 - 8  + 9
           (70 - 8 ) + 9
                62  + 9
                 71
```

24

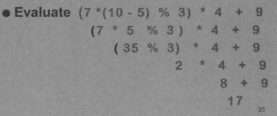

## Parentheses

- Parentheses can be used to change the usual order
- Parts in() are evaluated first
- Evaluate  $(7 * (10 - 5) \% 3) * 4 + 9$

$$(7 * 5 \% 3) * 4 + 9$$
$$(35 \% 3) * 4 + 9$$
$$2 * 4 + 9$$
$$8 + 9$$
$$17$$

25

### Recall Assignment Operator Syntax

Variable = Expression

- First, Expression on right is evaluated
- Then the resulting value is stored in the memory location of Variable on left

NOTE: An automatic type coercion occurs after evaluation but before the value is stored if the types differ for Expression and Variable

26

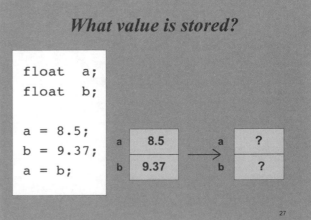

## *What value is stored?*

```
float  a;
float  b;

a = 8.5;
b = 9.37;
a = b;
```

| a | 8.5 |
|---|-----|
| b | 9.37 |

$\rightarrow$

| a | ? |
|---|---|
| b | ? |

27

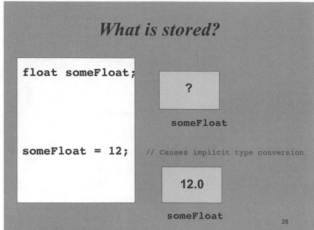

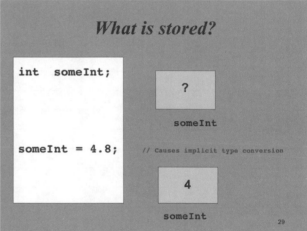

### Type Casting is Explicit Conversion of Type

| | | |
|---|---|---|
| int(4.8) | has value | 4 |
| float(5) | has value | 5.0 |
| float(7/4) | has value | 1.0 |
| float(7) / float(4) | has value | 1.75 |

## Notes

### Some Expressions

```
int  age;
```

| Example | | Value |
|---|---|---|
| age = 8 | | 8 |
| - age | | - 8 |
| 5 + 8 | | 13 |
| 5 / 8 | | 0 |
| 6.0 / 5.0 | | 1.2 |
| float(4 / 8) | 0.0 | |
| float(4) / 8 | 0.5 | |
| cout << "How old are you?" | | cout |
| cin  >>  age | | cin |
| cout << age | | cout |

31

### *What values are stored?*

```
float   loCost;
float   hiCost;

loCost = 12.342;
hiCost = 12.348;

loCost =
   float(int(loCost * 100.0 + 0.5)) / 100.0;

hiCost  =
   float(int(hiCost * 100.0 + 0.5)) / 100.0;
```

32

### Values were rounded to 2 decimal places

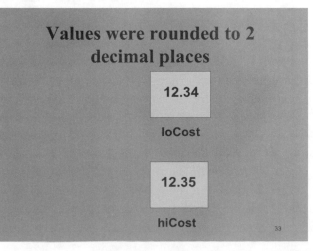

12.34

loCost

12.35

hiCost

33

**Notes**

### Functions

- Every C++ program must have a function called `main`

- Program execution always begins with function main

- Any other functions are subprograms and must be called

34

### Function Calls

- One function calls another by using the name of the called function together with() containing an argument list

- A function call temporarily transfers control from the calling function to the called function

35

### More About Functions

- It is not considered good practice for the body block of function main to be long

- Function calls are used to do subtasks

- Every C++ function has a return type

- If the return type is not void, the function returns a value to the calling block

36

# Notes

---

### Where are functions?

**Functions are subprograms**
- located in libraries, or
- written by programmers for their use in a particular program

37

---

| HEADER FILE | FUNCTION | EXAMPLE OF CALL | VALUE |
|---|---|---|---|
| <cstdlib> | abs(i) | abs(-6) | 6 |
| <cmath> | pow(x,y) | pow(2.0,3.0) | 8.0 |
| | fabs(x) | fabs(-6.4) | 6.4 |
| <cmath> | sqrt(x) | sqrt(100.0) | 10.0 |
| | sqrt(x) | sqrt(2.0) | 1.41421 |
| <cmath> | log(x) | log(2.0) | .693147 |
| <iomanip> | setprecision(n) | setprecision(3) | |

38

---

## Write C++ Expressions for

**The square root of $b^2 - 4ac$**

    sqrt(b * b - 4.0 * a * c)

**The square root of the average of myAge and yourAge**

    sqrt((myAge + yourAge) / 2)

39

---

## Function Call

- A function call temporarily transfers control to the called function's code

- When the function's code has finished executing, control is transferred back to the calling block

40

## Function Call Syntax

FunctionName =( Argument List )

The argument list is a way for functions to communicate with each other by passing information

The argument list can contain zero, one, or more arguments, separated by commas, depending on the function

41

## A void function call stands alone

```cpp
#include <iostream>

void  DisplayMessage(int  n);
// Declares function

int main()
{
    DisplayMessage(15);
    // Function call
    cout  <<  "Good Bye"  <<  endl;
    return 0;
}
```

42

## A void function does NOT return a value

```
// Header and body here

void  DisplayMessage(int  n)
{
    cout  <<  "I have liked math for  "
          <<  n  <<  " years"  <<  endl;
}
```

43

## Two Kinds of Functions

| Value-Returning | Void |
|---|---|
| Always returns a single value to its caller and is called from within an expression | Never returns a value to its caller and is called as a separate statement |

44

## << is a binary operator

<< is called the output or insertion operator

<< is left associative

| Expression | Has value |
|---|---|
| cout << age | cout |

**Statement**

```
cout << "You are "  << age  << " years old\n";
```

45

**Notes**

## \<iostream\> is header file

- For a library that defines 3 objects

  An istream object named cin (keyboard)

  An ostream object named cout (screen)

  An ostream object named cerr (screen)

46

## No I/O is built into C++

- Instead, a library provides input stream and output stream

Keyboard ➡ executing program ➡ Screen

istream      ostream

47

## Manipulators

- Manipulators are used only in input and output statements

- endl, fixed, showpoint, setw, and setprecision are manipulators that can be used to control output format

- endl is use to terminate the current output line and create blank lines in output

48

## Insertion Operator(<<)

- The insertion operator << takes 2 operands

- The left operand is a stream expression, such as cout

- The right operand is an expression of simple type, a string, or a manipulator

49

## Output Statements

SYNTAX(revised)

```
cout << ExpressionOrManipulator
      << ExpressionOrManipulator ...;
```

50

## Output Statements

SYNTAX

```
cout << Expression << Expression ...;
```

These examples yield the same output

```
cout << "The answer is ";
cout << 3 * 4;
```

```
cout << "The answer is " << 3 * 4;
```

51

**Notes**

## Using Manipulators
## Fixed and Showpoint

- use the following statement to specify that(for output sent to the cout stream) decimal format(not scientific notation) be used, and that a decimal point be included(even for floating values with 0 as fractional part)

  cout << fixed << showpoint;

52

## setprecision(n)

- Requires #include <iomanip> and appears in an expression using insertion operator(<<)

- If fixed has already been specified, argument n determines the number of places displayed after the decimal point for floating point values

- Remains in effect until explicitly changed by another call to setprecision

53

## What is exact output?

```
#include <iomanip> // For setw() and setprecision()
#include <iostream>

using namespace std;

int main()
{
    float   myNumber = 123.4587;
    cout << fixed <<   showpoint;
    // Use decimal format
    // Print decimal points
    cout << "Number is " << setprecision(3)
         << myNumber    << endl;

    return 0;
}
```

54

## OUTPUT

## Number is 123.459

Value is rounded if necessary to be displayed
with exactly 3 places after the decimal point

55

## Manipulator setw

- "Set width" lets us control how many character positions the next data item should occupy when it is output

- setw is only for formatting numbers and strings, not char type data

56

## setw(n)

- Requires #include <iomanip> and appears in an expression using insertion operator(<<)

- Argument n is called the fieldwidth specification, and determines the number of character positions in which to display a right-justified number or string(not char data); the number of positions used is expanded if n is too narrow

- "Set width" affects only the very next item displayed and is useful to align columns of output

57

**Notes**

### What is exact output?

```cpp
#include  <iomanip>              // For setw()
#include  <iostream>
#include  <string>

using  namespace  std;

int  main()
{
    int  myNumber   =  123;
    int  yourNumber =  5;

    cout <<  setw(10)  <<  "Mine"
         <<  setw(10)  <<  "Yours"  << endl
         <<  setw(10)  <<  myNumber
         <<  setw(10)  <<  yourNumber << endl;

    return 0;
}
```
58

### Output

position   12345678901234567890

```
      Mine      Yours
       123          5
```

Each is displayed right-justified and
each is located in a total of 10 positions

59

### What is exact output?

```cpp
#include  <iomanip> // For setw() and setprecision()
#include  <iostream>

using  namespace  std;

int  main()
{
    float myNumber   =  123.4;
    float yourNumber =  3.14159;

    cout  <<  fixed  << showpoint;
    // Use decimal format; print decimal points
    cout  <<  "Numbers are: "  <<  setprecision(4)
          <<  endl  <<  setw(10)  <<  myNumber
          <<  endl  <<  setw(10)  <<  yourNumber
          <<  endl;
    return 0;
}
```
60

50

Chapter 3

## OUTPUT

```
12345678901234567890
```

```
Numbers are:
  123.4000
    3.1416
```

Each is displayed right-justified and rounded if necessary and each is located in a total of 10 positions with 4 places after the decimal point

61

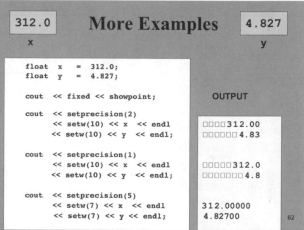

312.0

## More Examples

4.827

x                                                                y

```
float  x   =  312.0;
float  y   =  4.827;

cout  << fixed << showpoint;

cout  << setprecision(2)
      << setw(10) << x  << endl
      << setw(10) << y  << endl;

cout  << setprecision(1)
      << setw(10) << x  << endl
      << setw(10) << y  << endl;

cout  << setprecision(5)
      << setw(7) << x  << endl
      << setw(7) << y  << endl;
```

OUTPUT

```
□□□□312.00
□□□□□□4.83
```

```
□□□□□312.0
□□□□□□□4.8
```

```
312.00000
4.82700
```

62

| HEADER FILE | MANIPULATOR | ARGUMENT TYPE | EFFECT |
|---|---|---|---|
| <iostream> | endl | none | terminates output line |
| <iostream> | showpoint | none | displays decimal point |
| <iostream> | fixed | none | suppresses scientific notation |
| <iomanip> | setw(n) | int | sets fieldwidth to n positions |
| <iomanip> | setprecision(n) | int | sets precision to n digits |

63

### length Function

- Function `length` returns an unsigned integer value that equals the number of characters currently in the string

- Function `size` returns the same value as function length

- You must use dot notation in the call to function `length` or `size`

64

### find Function

- Function `find` returns an unsigned integer value that is the beginning position for the first occurrence of a particular substring within the string

- The substring argument can be a `string` constant, a `string` expression, or a `char` value

- If the substring was not found, function `find` returns the special value `string::npos`

65

### substr Function

- Function `substr` returns a particular substring of a string

- The first argument is an unsigned integer that specifies a starting position within the string

- The second argument is an unsigned integer that specifies the length of the desired substring

- Positions of characters within a string are numbered starting from 0, not from 1

66

## Mortgage Payments

**Problem** Your parents are thinking about refinancing their mortgage, and have asked you to help them with the calculations. Now that you're learning C++, you realize that you can save yourself a lot of calculator button-pressing by writing a program to do the calculations automatically.

67

## Algorithm

```
Define Constants
    Set LOAN_AMOUNT = 50000.00
    Set NUMBER_OF_YEARS = 7
    Set YEARLY_INTEREST = 0.0524
Calculate Values
    Set monthlyInterest to YEARLY_INTEREST divided by 12
    Set numberOfPayments to NUMBER_OF_YEARS times 12
    Set payment to(LOAN_AMOUNT *
        pow(monthlyInterest+1,numberrOfPayments)
        * monthlyInterest))
        /(pow(monthlyInterest+1, numberOfPayments) - 1)
Output Results
    Print "For a loan amount of " LOAN_AMOUNT "with an interest rate of "
        YEARLY_INTEREST " and a " NUMBER_OF_YEARS "
        year mortgage, "
    Print "your monthly payments are $" payment "."
```

68

## C++ Program

```cpp
//**************************************************
// Mortgage Payment Calculator program
// This program determines the monthly payments on a
// mortgage given the loan amount, the yearly interest,
// and the number of years.
//**************************************************
#include <iostream>          // Access cout
#include <cmath>             // Access power function
#include <iomanip>           // Access manipulators
using namespace std;
const float LOAN_AMOUNT = 50000.00;  // Amount of loan
const float YEARLY_INTEREST = 0.0524;// Yearly interest
const int NUMBER_OF_YEARS = 7;       // Number of years
```

69

## C++ Program

```cpp
int main()
{
    // Local variables
    float monthlyInterest; // Monthly interest rate
    int numberOfPayments;  // Total number of payments
    float payment;         // Monthly payment
    // Calculate values
    monthlyInterest = YEARLY_INTEREST / 12;
    numberOfPayments = NUMBER_OF_YEARS * 12;
    payment =(LOAN_AMOUNT *
        pow(monthlyInterest + 1, numberOfPayments)
        * monthlyInterest)/(pow(monthlyInterest + 1,
        numberOfPayments) - 1);
```

70

## C++ Program

```cpp
    // Output results
    cout << fixed << setprecision(2)
        << "For a loan amount of "
        << LOAN_AMOUNT  << " with an interest rate of "
        << YEARLY_INTEREST << " and a "
        << NUMBER_OF_YEARS
        << " year mortgage, " << endl;
    cout << " your monthly payments are $" << payment
        << "." << endl;
    return 0;
}
```

71

**Notes**

## Chapter 4 Topics

- Input Statements to Read Values into a Program using >>, and functions get, ignore, getline
- Prompting for Interactive Input/Output
- Using Data Files for Input and Output
- Object-Oriented Design Principles
- Functional Decomposition Methodology

## C++ Input/Output

- No built-in I/O in C++
- A library provides input stream and output stream

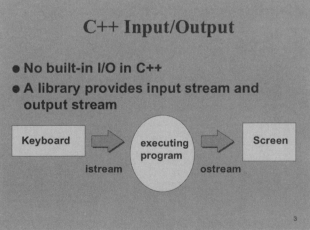

## <iostream>  Header File

**Access to a library that defines 3 objects**

- An istream object named cin (keyboard)

- An ostream object named cout (screen)

- An ostream object named cerr (screen)

4

## Giving a Value to a Variable

In your program you can assign(give) a value to the variable by using the assignment operator =

```
ageOfDog = 12;
```

or by another method, such as

```
cout << "How old is your dog?";
cin  >> ageOfDog;
```

5

## >> Operator

>> is called the input or extraction operator

>> is a binary operator

>> is left associative

| Expression | Has value |
|---|---|
| cin  >> age | cin |

Statement

```
cin  >>  age  >>  weight;
```

6

## Extraction Operator(>>)

- Variable cin is predefined to denote an input stream from the standard input device (the keyboard)

- The extraction operator >> called "get from" takes 2 operands; the left operand is a stream expression, such as cin--the right operand is a variable of simple type

- Operator >> attempts to extract the next item from the input stream and to store its value in the right operand variable

7

## Input Statements

SYNTAX

cin >> Variable >> Variable . . .;

These examples yield the same result.

cin >> length;
cin >> width;

cin >> length >> width;

8

## Whitespace Characters Include . . .

- blanks
- tabs
- end-of-line(newline) characters

The newline character is created by hitting Enter or Return at the keyboard, or by using the manipulator endl or "\n" in a program

9

**Notes**

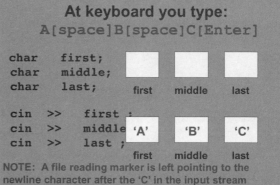

## Extraction Operator >>

>> "skips over" (actually reads but does not store anywhere) leading white space characters as it reads your data from the input stream(either keyboard or disk file)

10

## At keyboard you type:
### A[space]B[space]C[Enter]

```
char     first;
char     middle;
char     last;
```
first    middle    last

```
cin  >>  first ;
cin  >>  middle
cin  >>  last ;
```
'A'    'B'    'C'

first    middle    last

NOTE:  A file reading marker is left pointing to the newline character after the 'C' in the input stream

11

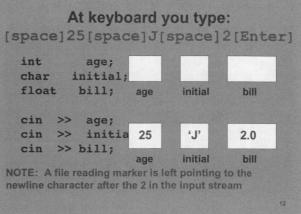

## At keyboard you type:
### [space]25[space]J[space]2[Enter]

```
int      age;
char     initial;
float    bill;
```
age    initial    bill

```
cin  >>  age;
cin  >>  initia
cin  >>  bill;
```
25    'J'    2.0

age    initial    bill

NOTE:  A file reading marker is left pointing to the newline character after the 2 in the input stream

12

**Notes**

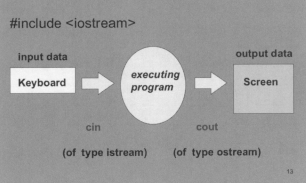

### Keyboard and Screen I/O

#include <iostream>

input data                    output data

Keyboard → executing program → Screen

cin             cout

(of type istream)     (of type ostream)

13

### Another example using >>

NOTE:    shows the location of the file reading marker

| STATEMENTS | CONTENTS | | | MARKER POSITION |
|---|---|---|---|---|
| int   i;<br>char  ch;<br>float  x; | | | | 25 A\n<br>16.9\n |
| | i | ch | x | |
| cin >> i; | 25 | | | 25 A\n<br>16.9\n |
| | i | ch | x | |
| cin >> ch; | 25 | 'A' | | 25 A\n<br>16.9\n |
| | i | ch | x | |
| cin >> x; | 25 | 'A' | 16.9 | 25 A\n<br>16.9\n |
| | i | ch | x | 14 |

### Another Way to Read char Data

The get() function can be used to read a single character.

get() obtains the very next character from the input stream without skipping any leading whitespace characters

15

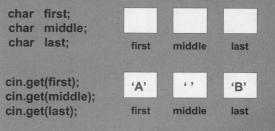

## At keyboard you type:
`A[space]B[space]C[Enter]`

```
char   first;
char   middle;
char   last;
```

|       |        |      |
|-------|--------|------|
| first | middle | last |

```
cin.get(first);
cin.get(middle);
cin.get(last);
```

| 'A'   | ' '    | 'B'  |
|-------|--------|------|
| first | middle | last |

NOTE: The file reading marker is left pointing to the space after the 'B' in the input stream

16

## Use function ignore() to skip characters

The ignore() function is used to skip(read and discard) characters in the input stream
The call

`cin.ignore(howMany, whatChar);`

will skip over up to **howMany** characters or until **whatChar** has been read, whichever comes first

17

## An Example Using cin.ignore()

NOTE:  ☐ shows the location of the file reading marker

| STATEMENTS | CONTENTS | | | MARKER POSITION |
|------------|----------|---|---|-----------------|
| int    a;<br>int    b;<br>int    c; | ☐<br>a | ☐<br>b | ☐<br>c | 957  34  1235\n<br>128  96\n |
| cin >> a >> b; | 957<br>a | 34<br>b | ☐<br>c | 957  34  **1235\n**<br>128  96\n |
| cin.ignore(100, '\n'); | 957<br>a | 34<br>b | ☐<br>c | 957  34  1235\n<br>**128**  96\n |
| cin >> c; | 957<br>a | 34<br>b | 128<br>c | 957  34  1235\n<br>128  **96\n** |

18

## Another Example Using cin.ignore()

NOTE:     shows the location of the file reading marker

| STATEMENTS | CONTENTS | | MARKER POSITION |
|---|---|---|---|
| int   i;<br>char  ch; | | | A 22 B 16 C 19\n |
| | i | ch | |
| cin >> ch; | | 'A' | A 22 B 16 C 19\n |
| | i | ch | |
| cin.ignore(100, 'B'); | | 'A' | A 22 B 16 C 19\n |
| | i | ch | |
| cin >> i; | 16 | 'A' | A 22 B 16 C 19\n |
| | i | ch | 19 |

## String Input in C++

Input of a string is possible using the extraction operator  >>

Example

```
string    message;
cin  >>   message;
Cout <<   message;
```

However . . .

20

## >> Operator with Strings

Using the extraction operator(>>)  to read input characters into a string variable

- The >> operator skips any leading whitespace characters such as blanks and newlines

- It then reads successive characters into the string, and stops at the first trailing whitespace character(which is not consumed, but remains waiting in the input stream)

21

## String Input Using >>

```
string    firstName;
string    lastName;
cin  >>  firstName >> lastName;
```

Suppose input stream looks like this:

☐☐Joe☐Hernandez☐23

*What are the string values?*

22

## Results Using >>

```
string    firstName;
string    lastName;
cin  >>  firstName >> lastName;
```

Result

| "Joe" | "Hernandez" |
|-------|-------------|
| firstName | lastName |

23

## getline() Function

- Because the extraction operator stops reading at the first trailing whitespace, >> cannot be used to input a string with blanks in it
- Use the getline function with 2 arguments to overcome this obstacle
- First argument is an input stream variable, and second argument is a string variable

Example

```
string    message;
getline(cin,  message);
```

24

## getline(inFileStream, str)

- getline does not skip leading whitespace characters such as blanks and newlines

- getline reads successive characters(including blanks) into the string, and stops when it reaches the newline character '\n'

- The newline is consumed by getline, but is not stored into the string variable

25

## String Input Using getline

```
string    firstName;
string    lastName;
getline(cin,  firstName);
getline(cin,  lastName);
```

Suppose input stream looks like this:

☐☐Joe☐Hernandez ☐23

*What are the string values?*

26

## Results Using getline

```
string    firstName;
string    lastName;
getline(cin,  firstName);
getline(cin,  lastName);
```

| " Joe Hernandez  23" | ? |
|---|---|
| firstName | lastName |

27

## Interactive I/O

- In an interactive program the user enters information while the program is executing

- Before the user enters data, a prompt should be provided to explain what type of information should be entered

- The amount of information needed in the prompt depends on
  - the complexity of the data being entered, and
  - the sophistication of the person entering the data

28

## Prompting for Interactive I/O

```
// Pattern: cout(prompt) cin(read value)
cout  <<  "Enter part number : "  <<  endl;
cin   >>  partNumber;
cout  <<  "Enter quantity ordered : "  <<  endl;
cin   >>  quantity;
cout  <<  "Enter unit price : "  <<  endl;
cin   >>  unitPrice;
// Calculate and print results
totalPrice  =  quantity * unitPrice;
cout  <<  "Part # "  <<  partNumber  <<  endl;
cout  <<  "Quantity: "  <<  quantity  <<  endl;
cout  <<  "Unit Cost: $ "  <<  setprecision(2)
      <<  unitPrice  <<  endl;
cout  <<  "Total Cost: $ "  <<  totalPrice  <<  endl;
```

29

## Disk Files for I/O

#include <fstream>

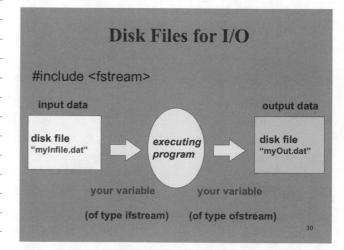

30

## Disk I/O

**To use** disk I/O

- Access #include <fstream>

- Choose valid identifiers for your filestreams and declare them

- Open the files and associate them with disk names

- Use your filestream identifiers in your I/O statements(using >> and << , manipulators, get, ignore)

- Close the files

31

## Disk I/O Statements

```
#include <fstream>

ifstream   myInfile;            // Declarations
ofstream   myOutfile;

myInfile.open("myIn.dat"); // Open files
myOutfile.open("myOut.dat");

myInfile.close();               // Close files
myOutfile.close();
```

32

## Opening a File

**Opening a file**

- Associates the C++ identifier for your file with the physical(disk) name for the file
    - If the input file does not exist on disk, open is not successful
    - If the output file does not exist on disk, a new file with that name is created
    - If the output file already exists, it is erased

- Places a file reading marker at the very beginning of the file, pointing to the first character in the file

33

## Stream Fail State

- When a stream enters the fail state,
  - Further I/O operations using that stream have no effect at all
  - The computer does not automatically halt the program or give any error message
- Possible reasons for entering fail state include
  - Invalid input data (often the wrong type)
  - Opening an input file that doesn't exist
  - Opening an output file on a disk that is already full or is write-protected

34

## Run Time File Name Entry

```
#include <string>
// Contains conversion function c_str

ifstream   inFile;
string     fileName;

cout << "Enter input file name: " << endl; // Prompt
cin   >>  fileName;

// Convert string fileName to a C string type
inFile.open(fileName.c_str());
```

35

## Functional Decomposition

A technique for developing a program in which the problem is divided into more easily handled subproblems, the solutions of which create a solution to the overall problem

In functional decomposition, we work from the abstract (a list of the major steps in our solution) to the particular (algorithmic steps that can be translated directly into code in C++ or another language)

36

## Functional Decomposition

Focus is on actions and algorithms

Begins by breaking the solution into a series of major steps; process continues until each subproblem cannot be divided further or has an obvious solution

Units are *modules* representing algorithms

- A module is a collection of concrete and abstract steps that solves a subproblem
- A module structure chart (hierarchical solution tree) is often created

Data plays a secondary role in support of actions to be performed

37

## Module Structure Chart

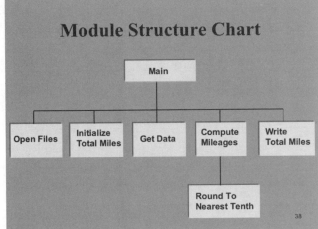

38

## Object-Oriented Design

A technique for developing a program in which the solution is expressed in terms of objects -- self-contained entities composed of data and operations on that data

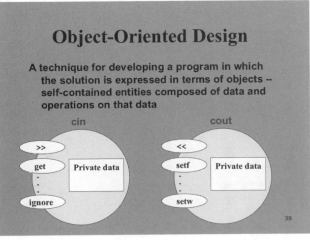

39

## More about OOD

- Languages supporting OOD include: C++, Java, Smalltalk, Eiffel, CLOS, and Object-Pascal

- A *class* is a programmer-defined data type and objects are variables of that type

- In C++, cin is an object of a data type (class) named istream, and cout is an object of a class ostream. Header files iostream and fstream contain definitions of stream classes

- A class generally contains private data and public operations (called *member functions*)

40

## Object-Oriented Design (OOD)

Focus is on entities called objects and operations on those objects, all bundled together

Begins by identifying the major objects in the problem, and choosing appropriate operations on those objects

Units are *objects*; programs are collections of objects that communicate with each other

Data plays a leading role; algorithms are used to implement operations on the objects and to enable object interaction

41

## Two Programming Methodologies

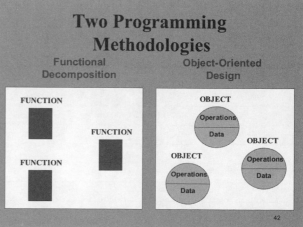

42

## Notes

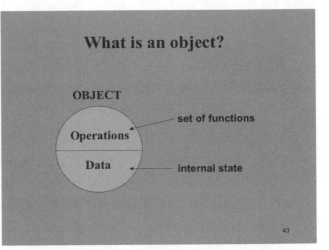

**What is an object?**

OBJECT

Operations — set of functions

Data — internal state

43

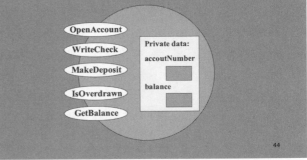

**An object contains data and operations**

checkingAccount

OpenAccount
WriteCheck
MakeDeposit
IsOverdrawn
GetBalance

Private data:
accoutNumber

balance

44

**OOD Used with Large Software Projects**

- Objects within a program often model real-life objects in the problem to be solved

- Many libraries of pre-written classes and objects are available as-is for re-use in various programs

- The OOD concept of inheritance allows the customization of an existing class to meet particular needs without having to inspect and modify the source code for that class--this can reduce the time and effort needed to design, implement, and maintain large systems

45

## Names in Multiple Formats

**Problem** You are beginning to work on a problem that needs to output names in several formats along with the corresponding social security number. As a start, you decide to write a short C++ program that inputs a social security number and a single name and displays it in the different formats, so you can be certain that all of your string expressions are correct.

46

## Algorithm

Main Module                                    Level 0
    Open files
    Get social security number
    Get name
    Write data in proper formats
    Close files
Open Files                                     Level 1
    inData.open("name.dat")
    outData.open("name.out")

47

Get Name
    Get first name
    Get middle name or initial
    Get last name
Write Data in Proper Formats
    Write first name, blank, middle name, blank,
      last name, blank, social security number
    Write last name, comma, first name, blank,
      middle name, blank, social security number
    Write last name, comma, blank, first name,
      blank, middle initial, period, blank,
      social security number
    Write first name, blank, middle initial, period,
      blank, last name

48

Middle initial                          Level 2
    Set initial to middleName.substr(0, 1) + period
Close files
    inData.close()
    outData.close()

49

# C++ Program

```
//**************************************************************
// Format Names program
// This program reads in a social security number, a first name
// a middle name or initial, and a last name from file inData.
// The name is written to file outData in three formats:
//    1. First name, middle name, last name, and social security
//    number.
//    2. last name, first name, middle name, and social
//    security number
//    3. last name, first name, middle initial, and social
//    security number
//    4.  First name, middle initial, last name
//**************************************************************
```

50

```cpp
#include <fstream>              // Access ofstream
#include <string>               // Access string
using namespace std;

int main()
{
    // Declare and open files
    ifstream inData;
    ofstream outData;
    inData.open("name.dat");
    outData.open("name.out");
    // Declare variables
    string socialNum;       // Social security number
    string firstName;       // First name
    string lastName;        // Last name
    string middleName;      // Middle name
    string initial;         // Middle initial
```

51

```cpp
    // Read in data from file inData
    inData >> socialNum >> firstName >> middleName
            >> lastName;
    // Access middle initial and append a period
    initial = middleName.substr(0, 1) + '.';
    // Output information in required formats
    outData << firstName << ' ' << middleName << ' '
            << lastName << ' ' << socialNum << endl;
    outData << lastName << ", " << firstName << ' '
            << middleName << ' ' << socialNum << endl;
    outData << lastName << ", " << firstName << ' '
            << initial << ' ' << socialNum << endl;
    outData << firstName << ' ' << initial << ' '
            << lastName;
    // Close files
    inData.close();
    outData.close();
    return 0;
}
```

52

# Chapter 5: Conditions, Logical Expressions, and Selection Control Structures

**Notes**

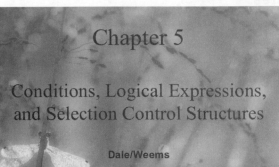

### Chapter 5

### Conditions, Logical Expressions, and Selection Control Structures

Dale/Weems

---

### Chapter 5 Topics

- Data Type bool
- Using Relational and Logical Operators to Construct and Evaluate Logical Expressions
- If-Then-Else Statements
- If-Then Statements
- Nested If Statements for Multi-way Branching
- Testing the State of an I/O Stream
- Testing a C++ Program

2

---

### Flow of Control

Flow of Control is the order in which program statements are executed

*What are the possibilities?*

3

## Flow of Control

- Sequential unless a "control structure" is used to change the order

- Two general types of control structures

    Selection (also called branching)

    Repetition (also called looping)

4

## bool Data Type

- Type bool is a built-in type consisting of just 2 values, the constants true and false

- We can declare variables of type bool

```
bool hasFever; // true if has high temperature
bool isSenior; // true if age is at least 55
```

5

## C++ Control Structures

- Selection
    if
    if . . . else
    switch

- Repetition
    for loop
    while loop
    do . . . while loop

6

**Notes**

---

## Expressions

**Control structures use** logical expressions **to make choices, which may include:**

*6 Relational Operators*

     <     <=    >     >=    ==    !=

*3 Logical Operators*

        !       &&      ||

7

---

## 6 Relational Operators

**are used in expressions of form:**

| *ExpressionA* | *Operator* | *ExpressionB* |
|---|---|---|
| temperature | > | humidity |
| rain | >= | average |
| B * B - 4.0 * A * C | < | 0.0 |
| hours | <= | 40 |
| abs (number) | == | 35 |
| initial | != | 'Q' |

8

---

Given
```
  int  x, y;
  x = 4;
  y = 6;
```

| Expression | Value |
|---|---|
| x < y | true |
| x + 2 < y | false |
| x != y | true |
| x + 3 >= y | true |
| y == x | false |
| y == x+2 | true |
| y = x + 3 | 7 (true) |

9

---

## Notes

---

### Comparing Strings

- Two objects of type string (or a string object and a C string) can be compared using the relational operators

- A character-by-character comparison is made using the ASCII character set values

- If all the characters are equal, then the 2 strings are equal. Otherwise, the string with the character with smaller ASCII value is the "lesser" string

10

---

```
string    myState;
string    yourState;

myState = "Texas";
yourState = "Maryland";
```

| Expression | Value |
|---|---|
| myState == yourState | false |
| myState > yourState | true |
| myState == "Texas" | true |
| myState < "texas" | true |

11

---

| Operator | Meaning | Associativity |
|---|---|---|
| ! | NOT | Right |
| *, / , % | Multiplication, Division, Modulus | Left |
| + , - | Addition, Subtraction | Left |
| < | Less than | Left |
| <= | Less than or equal to | Left |
| > | Greater than | Left |
| >= | Greater than or equal to | Left |
| == | Is equal to | Left |
| != | Is not equal to | Left |
| && | AND | Left |
| \|\| | OR | Left |
| = | Assignment | Right |

12

## Notes

_____

_____

_____

_____

_____

_____

_____

_____

_____

_____

_____

_____

_____

_____

_____

_____

_____

_____

_____

_____

_____

_____

_____

_____

_____

_____

_____

_____

_____

_____

_____

| Logical Expression | Meaning | Description |
|---|---|---|
| ! p | NOT p | ! p is false if p is true<br>! p is true if p is false |
| p && q | p AND q | p && q is true if both p and q are true. It is false otherwise. |
| p \|\| q | p OR q | p \|\| q is true if either p or q or both are true. It is false otherwise. |

13

```
int    age;
bool   isSenior,  hasFever;
float temperature;

age = 20;
temperature = 102.0;
isSenior = (age >= 55); // isSenior is  false
hasFever = (temperature > 98.6);
// hasFever is  true
```

| Expression | Value |
|---|---|
| isSenior && hasFever | false |
| isSenior \|\| hasFever | true |
| ! isSenior | true |
| ! hasFever | false |

14

### What is the value?

```
int age, height;

age = 25;
height = 70;
```

| Expression | Value |
|---|---|
| ! (age < 10) | ? |
| ! (height > 60) | ? |

15

**Notes**

## "Short-Circuit" Evaluation

- C++ uses short circuit evaluation of logical expressions

- This means logical expressions are evaluated left to right and evaluation stops as soon as the final truth value can be determined

16

## Short-Circuit Example

```
int age, height;
age = 25;
height = 70;
```

Expression

(age > 50)  &&  (height > 60)

false

Evaluation can stop now because result of && is only true when both sides are true; thus it is already determined that the expression will be false     17

## More Short-Circuiting

```
int  age, height;
age = 25;
height = 70;
```

Expression

(height > 60)  ||  (age > 40)

true

Evaluation can stop now because result of || is true if either side is true; thus it is already determined that the expression will be true     18

**Notes**

_____

## What happens?

```
int age, weight;

age = 25;
weight = 145;
```

_Expression_

(weight < 180)  &&  (age >= 20)

true

Must still be evaluated because truth
value of entire expression is not yet known
*(Why?)*

19

## What happens?

```
int  age, height;

age = 25;
height = 70;
```

_Expression_

! (height > 60)  ||  (age > 50)

true

false

*Does this part need to be evaluated?*  20

## Write an expression for each

taxRate is over 25% and income is less than
$20000

temperature is less than or equal to 75 or
humidity is less than 70%

age is over 21 and age is less than 60

age is 21 or 22

21

## Some Answers

```
(taxRate > .25) && (income < 20000)

(temperature <= 75) || (humidity < .70)

(age > 21) && (age < 60)

(age == 21) || (age == 22)
```

22

## Use Precedence Chart

```
int    number;
float  x;
```

number != 0 && x < 1 / number

| | |
|---|---|
| / | has highest priority |
| < | next priority |
| != | next priority |
| && | next priority |

*What happens if Number has value 0?*
  Run Time Error (Division by zero) occurs  23

## Short-Circuit Benefits

● One Boolean expression can be placed
  first to "guard" a potentially unsafe
  operation in a second Boolean
  expression

● Time is saved in evaluation of complex
  expressions using operators || and &&

24

## Notes

### Our Example Revisited

```
int    number;
float  x;

(number != 0)  &&  (x < 1 / number)
```

is evaluated first and has value false

Because operator is &&, the entire expression will have value false; because of short-circuiting, the right side is not evaluated in C++

25

### WARNING about Expressions in C++

- "Boolean expression" means an expression whose value is true or false
- An expression is any valid combination of operators and operands
- Each expression has a value, which can lead to unexpected results
- Construct your expressions carefully
  - use precedence chart to determine order
  - use parentheses for clarification (and safety)

26

### What went wrong?

This is only supposed to display "HEALTHY AIR" if the air quality index is between 50 and 80.

But when you tested it, it displayed "HEALTHY AIR" when the index was 35.

```
int  AQIndex;
AQIndex = 35;

if (50 < AQIndex < 80)
        cout << "HEALTHY AIR";
```

27

## Analysis of Situation

AQIndex = 35;

According to the precedence chart, the expression

(50 < AQIndex < 80)     *means*

(50 < AQIndex) < 80     *because < is Left Associative*

(50 < AQIndex) is false     *(has value 0)*

(0 < 80) is true.

28

## Corrected Version

```
int  AQIndex;
AQIndex = 35;

if ((50 < AQIndex) && (AQIndex < 80))
    cout << "HEALTHY AIR";
```

29

## Comparing Real Values

Do not compare floating point values for equality, compare them for near-equality.

```
float myNumber;
float yourNumber;

cin >> myNumber;
cin >> yourNumber;

if (fabs (myNumber - yourNumber) < 0.00001)
    cout << "They are close enough!"
        << endl;
```

30

**Notes**

### Flow of Control

Flow of control is the order in which program statements are executed

THE 3 POSSIBILITIES ARE:
Sequential
Selection Control Structure
Loop Control Structure

31

### Selection Statements

Selection statements are statements used to choose an action, depending on the current status of your program as it is running

32

### Expressions

Control structure use logical expressions which may include

6 Relational Operators

<    <=    >    >=    ==    !=

3 Logical Operators

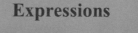

!    &&    | |

33

**Notes**

### What can go wrong here?

```
float   average;
float   total;
int     howMany;
  .
  .
  .
average = total / howMany;
```

34

### Improved Version

```
float   average,
float   total;
int     howMany;

if (howMany >  0)
{
    average = total   / howMany;
    cout <<  average;
}
else
    cout << "No prices were entered";
```

### If-Then-Else Syntax

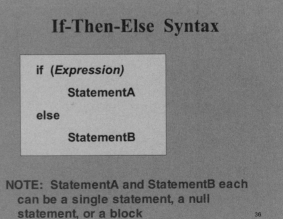

```
if (Expression)
        StatementA
else
        StatementB
```

NOTE:  StatementA and StatementB each
can be a single statement, a null
statement, or a block

36

**Notes**

_____
_____
_____
_____
_____
_____
_____
_____
_____
_____
_____
_____
_____
_____
_____
_____
_____
_____
_____
_____
_____
_____
_____
_____
_____
_____
_____
_____
_____
_____
_____
_____
_____
_____
_____
_____
_____

## if .. else provides two-way selection

**between executing one of 2 clauses (the if clause or the else clause)**

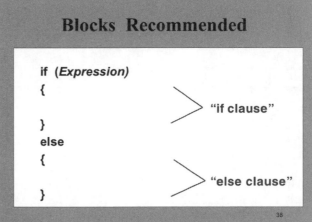

37

## Blocks Recommended

```
if (Expression)
{

}                              > "if clause"
else
{

}                              > "else clause"
```

38

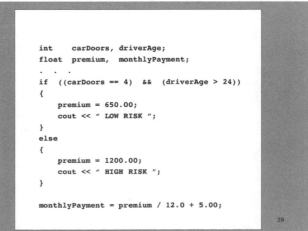

```
int     carDoors, driverAge;
float   premium,  monthlyPayment;
.  .  .
if  ((carDoors == 4)  &&  (driverAge > 24))
{
    premium = 650.00;
    cout << " LOW RISK ";
}
else
{
    premium = 1200.00;
    cout << " HIGH RISK ";
}

monthlyPayment = premium / 12.0 + 5.00;
```

39

## What happens if you omit braces?

```
if  ((carDoors == 4)  &&  (driverAge > 24))
     premium = 650.00;
     cout << " LOW RISK ";
else
     premium = 1200.00;
     cout << " HIGH RISK ";
monthlyPayment = premium / 12.0 + 5.00;
```

**Compile error occurs:  The "if clause" is the single statement following the if**

40

## Omitting Braces

**Braces can be omitted only when a clause is a single statement**

```
if (lastInitial  <= 'K')

    volume = 1;

else
    volume = 2;

cout  <<  "Look it up in volume # "
      <<  volume  <<  " of NYC phone book";
```

41

## Example

```
// Where is first 'A' found in a string?
string   myString;
string::size_type   pos;
  . . .
pos  =  myString.find('A');

if  (pos == string::npos)
    cout  <<  "No 'A' was found"  <<  endl;
else
    cout  <<  "An 'A' was found in position "
          <<  pos  <<  endl;
```

42

## Example

Assign value .25 to discountRate and assign value 10.00 to shipCost if purchase is over 100.00

Otherwise, assign value .15 to discountRate and assign value 5.00 to shipCost

Either way, calculate totalBill

43

## Example

```
Braces cannot be omitted!

if (purchase  >  100.00)
{
    discountRate  =  .25;
    shipCost  =  10.00;
}
else
{
    discountRate  =  .15;
    shipCost  =  5.00;
}

totalBill = purchase * (1.0 - discountRate) + shipCost;
```

44

## If-Then Statement

Determine whether or not to execute a statement (which can be a single statement or an entire block)

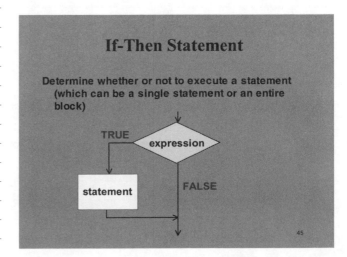

45

## If-Else Syntax

if *(Expression)*
    Statement

NOTE: Statement can be a single
statement, a null statement, or a block

46

## Example

```
// Stop processing if bad data
int   number;

cout  <<  "Enter a non-zero number ";
cin    >>    number;

if (number ==  0)
{
    cout  <<  "Bad input. Program terminated ";
    return 1;
}

// Otherwise continue processing
```

47

## These are equivalent. *Why?*

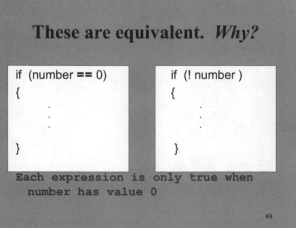

if (number == 0)          if (! number )
{                         {
    .                         .
    .                         .
    .                         .
}                         }

Each expression is only true when
number has value 0

48

## Notes

### Examples

If taxCode is 'T', increase price by adding taxRate times price to it

If code has value 1, read values for income and taxRate from myInfile, and calculate and display taxDue as their product

If A is strictly between 0 and 5, set B equal to 1/A, otherwise set B equal to A

49

### Some Answers

```
if   (taxCode == 'T')

    price = price + taxRate * price;
```

```
if (code == 1)
{
    myInfile >> income >> taxRate;
    taxDue = income * taxRate;
    cout << taxDue;
}
```

50

### Remaining Answer

```
if ((A > 0) && (A < 5))

    B = 1/A;

else

    B = A;
```

51

# Notes

### Example

**What is output? Why?**

```
int  age;

age = 20;

if  (age = 16)
{
    cout << "Did you get driver's license?";
}
```

52

### Example

**What is output? Why?**

```
int  age;

age =  30;

if  (age <  18)

    cout << "Do you drive?";
    cout << "Too young to vote";
```

53

### Example

**What is output? Why?**

```
int  code;

code =  0;

if  (! code)

    cout << "Yesterday";
else
    cout << "Tomorrow";
```

54

## Example

*What is output? Why?*

```
int  number;

number =  0;

if  (number =  0)

    cout << "Zero value";
else
    cout << "Non-zero value";
```

55

## Nested If Statements

```
if (Expression1 )
        Statement1
else if (Expression2 )
        Statement2
            .
            .
            .
else if (ExpressionN )
        StatementN
else
        Statement N+1
```

Exactly 1 of these statements will be executed    56

## Nested If Statements

Each Expression is evaluated in sequence, until
   some Expression is found that is true

Only the specific Statement following that particular
   true Expression is executed

If no Expression is true, the Statement following the
   final else is executed

Actually, the final else and final Statement are
   optional, and if omitted and no Expression is true,
   then no Statement is executed

An example . . .

57

## Multi-way Branching

```
if  (creditsEarned >= 90 )
    cout  <<  "SENIOR STATUS ";

else if  (creditsEarned >= 60 )
    cout  <<  "JUNIOR STATUS ";

else if  (creditsEarned >= 30 )
    cout  <<  "SOPHOMORE STATUS ";

else
    cout  <<  "FRESHMAN STATUS ";
```

## Example

Display one word to describe the int value of
number as "Positive", "Negative", or "Zero"

Your city classifies a pollution index
    less than 35 as "Pleasant",
    35 through 60 as "Unpleasant",
    above 60 as "Health Hazard"
    Display the correct description of the
    pollution index value

## One Answer

```
if (number >  0)

    cout << "Positive";

else if (number < 0)

    cout << "Negative";

else

    cout << "Zero";
```

## Other Answer

```
if (index < 35)

    cout << "Pleasant";

else if (index <= 60)

    cout << "Unpleasant";

else

    cout << "Health Hazard";
```

61

## Example

Write a void function  DisplayMessage that you can call from main to describe the pollution index value it receives as an argument

Your city describes a pollution index
    less than 35 as "Pleasant",
    35 through 60 as "Unpleasant",
    above 60 as "Health Hazard."

62

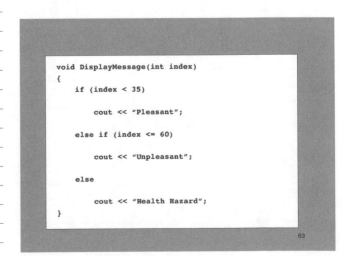

```
void DisplayMessage(int index)
{
    if (index < 35)

        cout << "Pleasant";

    else if (index <= 60)

        cout << "Unpleasant";

    else

        cout << "Health Hazard";
}
```

63

**Notes**

## A Driver Program

```
#include <iostream>

using namespace std;

void DisplayMessage (int);     // Declare function

int main (void)
{
    int pollutionIndex;        // Declare variable

    cout << "Enter air pollution index";
    cin >> pollutionIndex;
    DisplayMessage(pollutionIndex);  // Call
    return 0;
}
```
64

## Example

Every Monday thru Friday you go to class
    When it is raining you take an umbrella
But on the weekend, what you do
depends on the weather
    If it is raining you read in bed
    Otherwise, you have fun outdoors

65

## Solution

```
// Program tells how to spend your day
#include < iostream >
using namespace std;
void main (void)
{
    int     day;
    char    raining;
    cout << "Enter day (use 1 for Sunday)";
    cin  >>  day;
    cout << "Is it raining? (Y/N)";
    cin  >>  raining;
    if  ((day == 1) || (day == 7))
    { // Sat or Sun
        if (raining == 'Y')
            cout << "Read in bed";
        else
            cout << "Have fun outdoors";
    }
    else
    {
        cout << "Go to class ";
        if (raining == 'Y')
            cout << "Take an umbrella";
    }
}
```

## In the absence of braces,

an `else` is always paired with the closest preceding `if` that doesn't already have an `else` paired with it

67

## Example

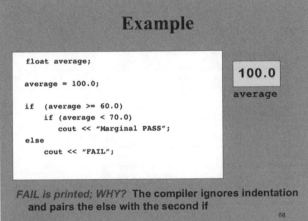

```
float average;

average = 100.0;

if   (average >= 60.0)
     if (average < 70.0)
        cout << "Marginal PASS";
else
     cout << "FAIL";
```

100.0
average

*FAIL is printed; WHY?* The compiler ignores indentation and pairs the else with the second if

68

## To correct the problem, use braces

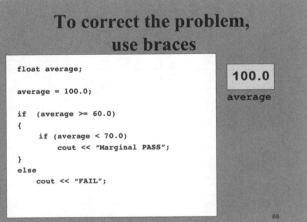

```
float average;

average = 100.0;

if   (average >= 60.0)
{
     if (average < 70.0)
        cout << "Marginal PASS";
}
else
     cout << "FAIL";
```

100.0
average

69

## Each I/O stream has a state (condition)

- An input stream enters fail state when you
  try to read invalid input data
  try to open a file which does not exist
  try to read beyond the end of the file

- An output stream enters fail state when you
  try to create a file with an invalid name
  try to create a file on a write-protected disk
  try to create a file on a full disk

70

## Determining the Stream State

- The stream identifier can be used as if it were a Boolean variable that has value false when the last I/O operation on that stream failed and true when it did not fail
- After you use a file stream, you should check on its state

71

## Checking the State

```
ofstream  myOutfile;

myOutfile.open ("myOut.dat");

if  (! myOutfile)
{
  cout  <<  "File opening  error.  "
       <<  "Program terminated."  <<  endl;
  return 1;
}
            // Otherwise send output to myOutfile
```

72

## Testing Selection Control Structures

- To test a program with branches, use enough data sets to ensure that every branch is executed at least once

- This strategy is called minimum complete coverage

73

## Testing Often Combines Two Approaches

| WHITE BOX TESTING | BLACK BOX TESTING |
|---|---|
| **Code Coverage** | **Data Coverage** |
| Allows us to see the program code while designing the tests, so that data values at the boundaries, and possibly middle values, can be tested. | Tries to test as many allowable data values as possible without regard to program code. |

74

## Testing

- Design and implement a test plan

- A test plan is a document that specifies the test cases to try, the reason for each, and the expected output

- Implement the test plan by verifying that the program outputs the predicted results

75

| PHASE | RESULT | TESTING TECHNIQUE |
|---|---|---|
| Problem solving | Algorithm | Algorithm walk-through |
| Implementation | Coded program | Code walk-through, Trace |
| Compilation | Object program | Compiler messages |
| Execution | Output | Implement test plan |

76

## Body Mass Index Problem

**Problem** Implement a measure called the Body Mass Index (BMI), which computes a ratio of your weight and height, which has become a popular tool to determine an appropriate weight. The formula for non-metric values is

$$BMI = weight * 703 / height^2$$

77

## *What is the BMI?*

BMI correlates with body fat, which can be used to determine if a weight is unhealthy for a certain height. Do a search of the Internet for "body mass index" and you will find more than a million hits. In these references, the formula remains the same but the interpretation varies somewhat, depending on age and sex. Here is a the most commonly used generic interpretation.

| BMI | Interpretation |
|---|---|
| < 20 | Underweight |
| 20-25 | Normal |
| 26-30 | Overweight |
| over 30 | Obese |

78

## Algorithm

Get Data                                    Level 1
    Prompt for weight
    Read weight
    Prompt for height
    Read height
Test Data
    IF weight < 0 OR  height < 0
      Set dataAreOK to false
    ELSE
      Set dataAreOK to true
Calculate  BMI
    Set bodyMassIndex to weight * 703 / height $^2$

79

## Algorithm Continued

Print
    Print "Your BMI is ", bodyMassIndex,  '.'
    Print "Interpretation and instructions."
    IF bodyMassIndex <20
      Print "Underweight: Have a milk shake."
    ELSE IF bodyMassIndex < 26
      Print "Normal: Have a glass of milk."
    ELSE IF bodyMassIndex < 30
      Print "Overweight: Have a glass of iced tea."
    ELSE
      Print "Obese: See your doctor."

80

## C++ Program

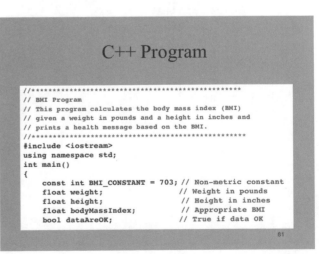

```
//***************************************************
// BMI Program
// This program calculates the body mass index (BMI)
// given a weight in pounds and a height in inches and
// prints a health message based on the BMI.
//***************************************************
#include <iostream>
using namespace std;
int main()
{
    const int BMI_CONSTANT = 703; // Non-metric constant
    float weight;                 // Weight in pounds
    float height;                 // Height in inches
    float bodyMassIndex;          // Appropriate BMI
    bool dataAreOK;               // True if data OK
```

81

```
    // Calculate body mass index
    bodyMassIndex = weight * BMI_CONSTANT
            / (height * height);
    // Print message indicating status
    cout << "Your BMI is "
        << bodyMassIndex << ". " << endl;
    cout << "Interpretation and instructions. "
        << endl;
    if (bodyMassIndex < 20)
        cout << "Underweight: ...." << endl;
    else if (bodyMassIndex <= 25)
        cout << "Normal: ...."   << endl;
    else if (bodyMassIndex <= 30)
        cout << "Overweight:...."  << endl;
    else
        cout << "Obese: ...." << endl;
    return 0;
}
```

82

## Testing the BMI Program

There is no testing in this program, but there should be!!

- *Should you use white box or black box testing?*
- *What test should be included?*
- *Where should they be inserted?*

83

# Chapter 6: Looping

**Notes**

**Chapter 6 Topics**

- While Statement Syntax
- Count-Controlled Loops
- Event-Controlled Loops
- Using the End-of-File Condition to Control Input Data
- Using a While Statement for Summing and Counting
- Nested While Loops
- Loop Testing and Debugging

2

**Loops**

*What is a loop?*

A loop is a repetition control structure that causes a single statement or block to be executed repeatedly

3

## Two Types of Loops

**Count controlled loops**

Repeat a statement or block a specified number of times

**Event-controlled loops**

Repeat a statement or block until a condition within the loop body changes that causes the repetition to stop

4

## While Statement

SYNTAX

```
while (Expression)
{      .
       .                    // loop body
       .
}
```

Loop body can be a single statement, a null statement, or a block

5

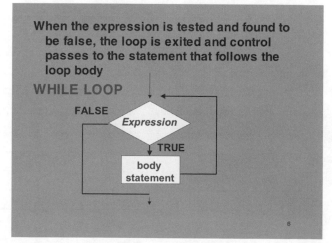

When the expression is tested and found to be false, the loop is exited and control passes to the statement that follows the loop body

WHILE LOOP

6

## Count-Controlled Loops

**Count-controlled loops contain**

- An *initialization* of the loop control variable
- An *expression* to test if the proper number of repetitions has been completed
- An *update* of the loop control variable to be executed with each iteration of the body

7

## Count-Controlled Loop Example

```
int    count;        // Loop-control variable

count = 4;           // Initialize loop variable

while(count > 0)     // Test expression
{
    cout << count << endl; // Repeated action

    count --;        // Update loop variable
}
cout << "Done" << endl;
```

8

## Count-controlled Loop

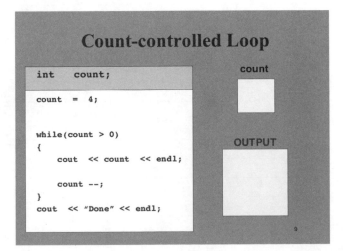

```
int    count;

count = 4;


while(count > 0)
{
    cout << count << endl;

    count --;
}
cout << "Done" << endl;
```

count

OUTPUT

9

# Notes

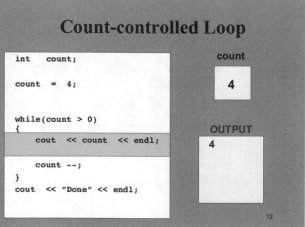

### Count-controlled Loop

```
int    count;

count  =  4;


while(count > 0)
{
    cout  << count  << endl;

    count --;
}
cout  << "Done" << endl;
```

count

**4**

OUTPUT

10

### Count-controlled Loop

```
int    count;

count  =  4;

while(count > 0)   TRUE
{
    cout  << count  << endl;

    count --;
}
cout  << "Done" << endl;
```

count

**4**

OUTPUT

11

### Count-controlled Loop

```
int    count;

count  =  4;

while(count > 0)
{
    cout  << count  << endl;

    count --;
}
cout  << "Done" << endl;
```

count

**4**

OUTPUT

4

12

**Notes**

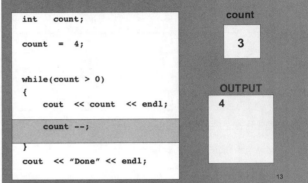

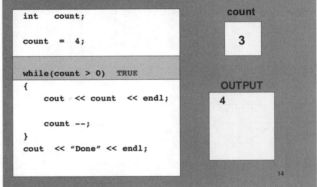

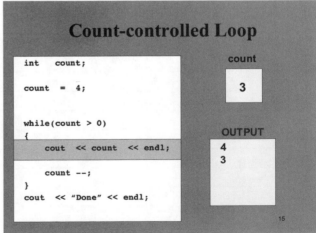

## Notes

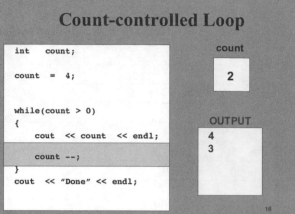

### Count-controlled Loop

```
int    count;

count  =  4;


while(count > 0)
{
    cout  << count  << endl;

    count --;
}
cout  << "Done" << endl;
```

count

`2`

OUTPUT

`4`
`3`

18

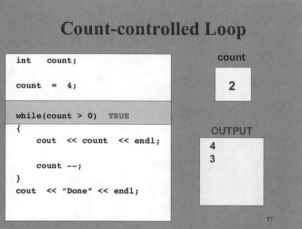

### Count-controlled Loop

```
int    count;

count  =  4;

while(count > 0)    TRUE
{
    cout  << count  << endl;

    count --;
}
cout  << "Done" << endl;
```

count

`2`

OUTPUT

`4`
`3`

17

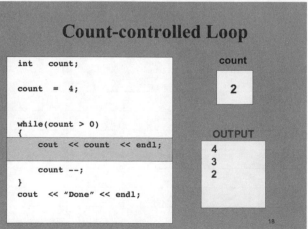

### Count-controlled Loop

```
int    count;

count  =  4;

while(count > 0)
{
    cout  << count  << endl;

    count --;
}
cout  << "Done" << endl;
```

count

`2`

OUTPUT

`4`
`3`
`2`

18

**Notes**

### Count-controlled Loop

```
int   count;

count  =  4;


while(count > 0)
{
    cout  << count  << endl;

    count --;
}
cout  << "Done" << endl;
```

count

**1**

OUTPUT

4
3
2

19

### Count-controlled Loop

```
int   count;

count  =  4;

while(count > 0)   TRUE
{
    cout  << count  << endl;

    count --;
}
cout  << "Done" << endl;
```

count

**1**

OUTPUT

4
3
2

20

### Count-controlled Loop

```
int   count;

count  =  4;

while(count > 0)
{
    cout  << count  << endl;

    count --;
}
cout  << "Done" << endl;
```

count

**1**

OUTPUT

4
3
2
1

21

## Notes

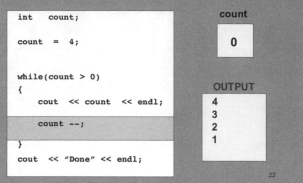

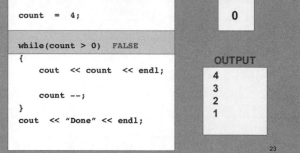

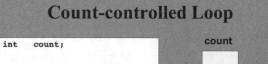

**Notes**

_____

_____

_____

_____

_____

_____

_____

_____

_____

_____

_____

_____

_____

_____

_____

_____

_____

_____

_____

_____

_____

_____

_____

_____

_____

_____

_____

_____

_____

_____

_____

_____

_____

_____

_____

### Example

**myInfile contains 100 blood pressures**

**Use a while loop to read the 100 blood pressures and find their total**

25

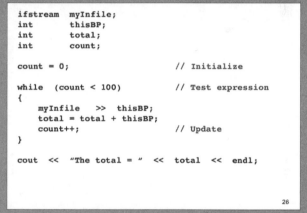

```
ifstream  myInfile;
int       thisBP;
int       total;
int       count;

count = 0;                    // Initialize

while  (count < 100)          // Test expression
{
    myInfile  >>  thisBP;
    total = total + thisBP;
    count++;                  // Update
}

cout  <<  "The total = "  <<  total  <<  endl;
```

26

### Types of Event-Controlled Loops

- **Sentinel controlled**
  **Keep processing data until a special value that is not a possible data value is entered to indicate that processing should stop**

- **End-of-file controlled**
  **Keep processing data as long as there is more data in the file**

- **Flag controlled**
  **Keep processing data until the value of a flag changes in the loop body**

27

## Notes

### Examples of Kinds of Loops

| Count controlled loop | Read exactly 100 blood pressures from a file |
|---|---|
| End-of-file controlled loop | Read all the blood pressures from a file no matter how many are there |

28

### Examples of Kinds of Loops

| Sentinel controlled loop | Read blood pressures until a special value selected by you(like -1) is read |
|---|---|
| Flag controlled loop | Read blood pressures until a dangerously high BP(200 or more) is read |

29

### A Sentinel-controlled Loop

- Requires a "priming read"

- A priming read is the reading of one set of data before the loop to initialize the variables in the expression

30

# Notes

```
// Sentinel controlled loop

total = 0;

cout  <<  "Enter a blood pressure(-1 to stop) ";
cin  >> thisBP;


while(thisBP != -1)        // While not sentinel
{
    total = total + thisBP;
    cout  <<  "Enter a blood pressure(-1 to stop)";
    cin >> thisBP;
}
cout  << total;
```
31

## End-of-File Controlled Loop

● Uses the fact that a file goes into the
fail state when you try to read a data
value beyond the end of the file to
control the loop

32

```
// End-of-file controlled loop

 total = 0;

 myInfile  >>  thisBP;            // Priming read


 while(myInfile)      // While last read successful
 {
     total = total + thisBP;
     myInfile  >>  thisBP;        // Read another
 }

 cout  <<  total;
```
33

# Notes

```
// End-of-file at keyboard

total = 0;

cout   << "Enter blood pressure "
       << "(Ctrl-Z to stop)";
cin  >> thisBP;          // Priming read

while(cin)    // While last read successful
{
    total = total + thisBP;
    cout   << "Enter blood pressure";
    cin >> thisBP;     // Read another
}
cout << total;
```
34

## Flag-controlled Loops

- Initialize a flag(to true or false)
- Use meaningful name for the flag
- A condition in the loop body changes the value of the flag
- Test for the flag in the loop test expression

35

```
countGoodReadings = 0;
isSafe = true;      // Initialize Boolean flag

while(isSafe)
{
    cin  >>  thisBP;
    if (thisBP >=  200)
        isSafe = false;  // Change flag value

    else
        countGoodReadings++;
}

cout  <<  countGoodReadings  <<   endl;
```
36

**Notes**

## Common Loop Uses

- Count all data values

- Count special data values

- Sum data values

- Keep track of current and previous values

37

## Current and Previous Values

- Write a program that counts the number of != operators in a program file

- Read one character in the file at a time

- Keep track of current and previous characters

38

## Keeping Track of Values

```
(x != 3)
{
   cout << endl;
}
```

FILE CONTENTS

| previous | current | count |
|----------|---------|-------|
| ( | x | 0 |
| x | ' ' | 0 |
| ' ' | ! | 0 |
| ! | = | 1 |
| = | ' ' | 1 |
| ' ' | 3 | 1 |
| 3 | ) | 1 |

39

**Notes**

```
int    count;
char   previous;
char   current;

count = 0;
inFile.get(previous);          // Priming reads
inFile.get(current);

while(inFile)
{
    if((current == '=') && (previous == '!'))
        count++;
    previous = current;        // Update
    inFile.get(current);       // Read another
}
```
40

## Nested Loops

```
initialize outer loop
while (outer loop condition)
{       . . .

        initialize inner loop
        while(inner loop condition)
        {
                inner loop processing and update
        }

        . . .
}
```
41

## Patient Data

A file contains blood pressure data for different people. Each line has a patient ID, the number of readings for that patient, followed by the actual readings.

| ID | howMany | Readings | | | | |
|------|---------|-----|-----|-----|-----|-----|
| 4567 | 5 | 180 | 140 | 150 | 170 | 120 |
| 2318 | 2 | 170 | 210 | | | |
| 5232 | 3 | 150 | 151 | 151 | | |

42

## Read the data and display a chart

| Patient ID | BP Average |
|------------|------------|
| 4567       | 152        |
| 2318       | 190        |
| 5232       | 151        |
| .          | .          |
| .          | .          |
| .          | .          |

There were 432 patients in file.

43

## Algorithm

Initialize patientCount to 0
Read first ID and howMany from file
While not end-of-file
    Increment patientCount
    Display ID
    Read and sum this patient's BP's
    Calculate and display average for patient
    Read next ID and howMany from file
display patientCount

44

## Designing Nested Loops

- Begin with outer loop

- When you get to where the inner loop appears, make it a separate module and come back to its design later

45

# Notes

```
#include <iostream>
#include <fstream>

using namespace std;

int  main()
{
    int patientCount; // Declarations
    int thisID;
    int howMany;
    int thisBP;
    int totalForPatient;
    int count;

    float average;

    ifstream  myInfile;
```
46

```
    myInfile.open("BP.dat");

    if (!myInfile)       // Opening failed
    {
        cout <<
          "File opening error. Program terminated.";
        return  1;
    }

    cout << "ID Number Average BP" << endl;

    patientCount = 0;

    myInfile >> thisID >> howMany; // Priming read
```
47

```
    while(myInfile)             // Last read successful
    {
        patientCount++;
        cout << thisID;
        totalForPatient = 0; // Unitialize inner loop
        count = 0;
        while(count < howMany)
        {
            myInfile >> thisBP;
            count ++;
            totalForPatient =
                totalForPatient  + thisBP;
        }

        average = totalForPatient / float(howMany);
        cout  <<  int(average + .5) << endl;
        // Another read
        myInfile  >> thisID  >>  howMany;
    }
```
48

```
        cout <<    "There were " <<    patientCount
             <<    "patients on file." << endl;

        cout <<    "Program terminated."  << endl;

        return 0;
}
```

49

## Information About 20 Books in Diskfile

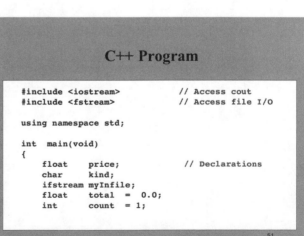

"myIn.dat"

Price of book                                    Hardback or
                                                 Paperback?

```
3.98  P <eoln>
7.41  H <eoln>
8.79  P <eoln>
```

Write a program to find total value of all books

50

## C++ Program

```
#include <iostream>               // Access cout
#include <fstream>                // Access file I/O

using namespace std;

int  main(void)
{
    float    price;               // Declarations
    char     kind;
    ifstream myInfile;
    float    total  =  0.0;
    int      count  = 1;
```

51

## C++ Program

```
myInfile.open("myIn.dat");

// count-controlled processing loop
while( count <= 20)
{
    myInfile  >>  price  >>  kind;
    total = total + price;
    count ++;
}
cout << "Total is: " << total << endl;
myInfile.close();
return 0;
}
```

52

## Trace of Program Variables

| count | price | kind | total |
|-------|-------|------|-------|
|       |       |      | 0.0   |
| 1     | 3.98  | 'P'  | 3.98  |
| 2     | 7.41  | 'H'  | 11.39 |
| 3     | 8.79  | 'P'  | 20.18 |
| 4     | etc.  |      |       |
|       |       |      |       |
| 20    |       |      |       |
| 21    | so loop terminates | | |

53

## Complexity

- Complexity is a measure of the amount of work involved in executing an algorithm relative to the size of the problem

54

## Polynomial Times

| N | $N^0$ constant | $N^1$ linear | $N^2$ quadratic | $N^3$ cubic |
|---|---|---|---|---|
| 1 | 1 | 1 | 1 | 1 |
| 10 | 1 | 10 | 100 | 1,000 |
| 100 | 1 | 100 | 10,000 | 1,000,000 |
| 1,000 | 1 | 1,000 | 1,000,000 | 1,000,000,000 |
| 10,000 | 1 | 10,000 | 100,000,000 | 1,000,000,000,000 |

55

## Loop Testing and Debugging

- Test data should test all sections of program

- Beware of infinite loops – program doesn't stop

- Check loop termination condition, and watch for "off-by-1" bugs(OBOBs)

- Use get function for loops controlled by detection of '\n' character

- Use algorithm walk-through to verify pre- and postconditions

- Trace execution of loop by hand with code walk-through

- Use a debugger to run program in "slow motion" or use debug output statements

56

**Notes**

## Chapter 7 Topics

- Writing a Program Using Functional Decomposition
- Writing a Void Function for a Task
- Using Function Arguments and Parameters
- Differences between Value Parameters and Reference Parameters
- Using Local Variables in a Function
- Function Preconditions and Postconditions

2

## Functions

- Every C++ program must have a function called `main`

- Program execution always begins with function `main`

- Any other functions are subprograms that must be explicitly called

3

## Function Calls

One function calls another by using the name of the called function followed by()s that enclose an argument list, which may be empty

A function call temporarily transfers control from the calling function to the called function

4

## Function Call Syntax

FunctionName( Argument List )

The argument list is a way for functions to communicate with each other by passing information

The argument list can contain 0, 1, or more arguments, separated by commas, depending on the function

5

## Two Parts of Function Definition

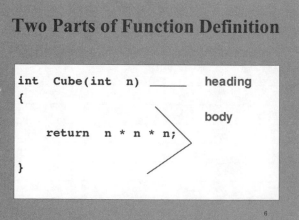

```
int  Cube(int  n) _____  heading
{
        return  n * n * n;         body
}
```

6

**Notes**

_____
_____
_____
_____
_____
_____
_____
_____
_____
_____
_____
_____
_____
_____
_____
_____
_____
_____
_____
_____
_____
_____
_____
_____
_____
_____
_____
_____
_____
_____
_____
_____
_____
_____
_____
_____
_____

## What is in a heading?

type of value returned

name of function

parameter list

```
int Cube (int n)
```

7

## Prototypes

**A prototype looks like a heading but must end with a semicolon, and its parameter list needs only to contain the type of each parameter**

```
int  Cube(int );   // Prototype
```

8

## Function Calls

When a function is called, temporary memory is allocated for its value parameters, any local variables, and for the function's name if the return type is not void

Flow of control then passes to the first statement in the function's body

The called function's statements are executed until a return statement (with or without a return value) or the closing brace of the function body is encountered

Then control goes back to where the function was called

9

```
#include <iostream>
int Cube(int);      // prototype
using namespace std;

void  main()
{
    int        yourNumber;
    int        myNumber;
    yourNumber = 14;
    myNumber   =  9;
    cout << "My Number = " << myNumber;
    cout << "its cube is " << Cube(myNumber) << endl;
    cout << "Your Number = " << yourNumber;
    cout << "its cube is " << Cube(yourNumber)
        << endl;
}
                                arguments
```

10

## Successful Function Compilation

Before a function is called in your
    program, the compiler must have
    previously processed either the
    function's prototype or the
    function's definition (heading and
    body)

11

## Return Values

In C++, a value-returning function
    returns in its identifier one value of
    the type specified in its heading and
    prototype (called the return type)

In contrast, a void-function cannot
    return any value in its identifier

12

## Example

Write a void function called
DisplayMessage(), which you can call
from main(), to describe the pollution
index value it receives as a parameter

Your city describes a pollution index
less than 35 as "Pleasant",
35 through 60 as "Unpleasant",
and above 60 as "Health Hazard"

13

parameter

```cpp
void DisplayMessage(int index)

{
    if(index < 35)
        cout << "Pleasant";
    else if(index <= 60)
        cout << "Unpleasant";
    else
        cout << "Health Hazard";
}
```

14

## The Rest of the Program

```cpp
#include <iostream>
void DisplayMessage(int);              // Prototype
using namespace std;

int main()
{
    int pollutionIndex;

    cout << "Enter air pollution index";
    cin >> pollutionIndex;
    DisplayMessage(pollutionIndex);  // Call
    return 0;
}
                    argument
```

15

## Return Statement

```
return;  // No value to return
```

- Is valid only in the body block of a void function

- Causes control to leave the function and immediately return to the calling block, leaving any subsequent statements in the function body unexecuted

16

## Header Files

Header Files contain
- Named constants like
  const int INT_MAX = 32767;

- Function prototypes like
  float sqrt(float);

- Classes like
  string, ostream, istream

- Objects like
  cin, cout

17

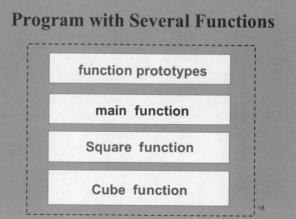

## Program with Several Functions

| function prototypes |
| main function |
| Square function |
| Cube function |

18

## Notes

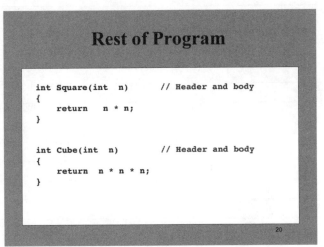

### Value-Returning Functions

```
#include <iostream>

int  Square(int);            // Prototypes
int  Cube(int);
using namespace std;

int  main()
{
    cout << "The square of 27 is "
         << Square(27) << endl;
    cout <<  "The cube of 27 is "
         << Cube(27)  << endl;
    return 0;
}
              function calls
```
19

### Rest of Program

```
int Square(int  n)      // Header and body
{
    return   n * n;
}


int Cube(int  n)        // Header and body
{
    return   n * n * n;
}
```
20

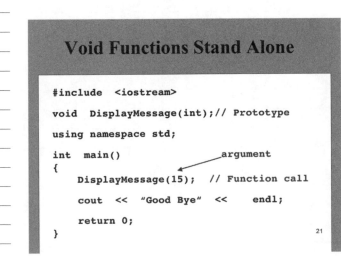

### Void Functions Stand Alone

```
#include  <iostream>

void  DisplayMessage(int);// Prototype

using namespace std;

int  main()                      argument
{
    DisplayMessage(15);  // Function call

    cout  <<  "Good Bye"  <<     endl;

    return 0;
}
```
21

## Parameters

```
                                          parameter
void  DisplayMessage(int  n)
{
    cout << "I have liked math for  "
         << n  <<  " years"
         << endl;

    return;
}
```
22

## Parameter List

A parameter list is the means used
for a function to share
information with the block
containing the call

23

## Classified by Location

| Arguments | Parameters |
|-----------|-----------|
| Always appear in a function call within the calling block | Always appear in the function heading, or function prototype |

24

## Different Terms

**Some C++ books**
- Use the term "actual parameters" for arguments

- Those books then refer to parameters as "formal parameters"

25

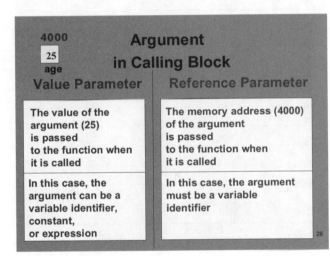

**4000**

**25**
**age**

## Argument in Calling Block

| Value Parameter | Reference Parameter |
|---|---|
| The value of the argument (25) is passed to the function when it is called | The memory address (4000) of the argument is passed to the function when it is called |
| In this case, the argument can be a variable identifier, constant, or expression | In this case, the argument must be a variable identifier |

26

## Default Parameters

- Simple types, structs, and classes are value parameters by default
- Arrays are always reference parameters
- Other reference parameters are marked as such by having an ampersand(&) beside their type

27

**Notes**

## Use of Reference Parameters

Reference parameters should be used when the function is to assign a value to, or change the value of, a variable from the calling block without an assignment statement in the calling block

28

## Using a Reference Parameter

● Is like giving someone the key to your home

● The key can be used by the other person to change the contents of your home!

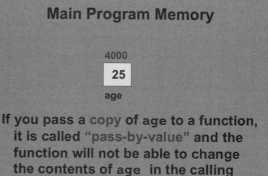

29

## Main Program Memory

4000

**25**

age

If you pass a copy of age to a function, it is called "pass-by-value" and the function will not be able to change the contents of age in the calling block; it is still 25 when you return

30

### Main Program Memory

4000

**25**

age

**BUT, if you pass 4000, the address of age to a function, it is called "pass-by-reference" and the function will be able to change the contents of age in the calling block; it could be 23 or 90 when you return**

31

### Additional Terms

● **Pass-by-reference is also called . . .**
 ■ pass-by-address, or
 ■ pass-by-location

 *Can you explain why?*

32

### Example of Pass-by-Reference

We want to find 2 real roots for a quadratic equation with coefficients a,b,c. Write a prototype for a void function named GetRoots() with 5 parameters. The first 3 parameters are type float. The last 2 are reference parameters of type float.

33

// Prototype

```
void GetRoots(float, float, float,
    float&, float&);
```

Now write the function definition using this information

This function uses 3 incoming values a, b, c from the calling block. It calculates 2 outgoing values root1 and root2 for the calling block. They are the 2 real roots of the quadratic equation with coefficients a, b, c.

34

## Function Definition

```
void  GetRoots(float a,  float b,  float c,
               float& root1, float& root2)
{
    float temp;                    // Local variable

    temp = b * b - 4.0 * a * c;

    root1 =(-b + sqrt(temp)) /(2.0 * a);

    root2 =(-b - sqrt(temp)) /(2.0 * a);

    return;
}
```
35

```
#include <iostream>
#include <fstream>
#include <cmath>
// Prototype
void GetRoots(float, float, float, float&, float&);
using namespace std;
void main()
{
    ifstream myInfile;
    ofstream myOutfile;
    float a, b, c, first, second;
    int count = 0;
    ......                              // Open files
    while(count <  5)
    {   myInfile >> a >> b >> c;
        GetRoots(a, b, c, first, second);  // Call
        myOutfile << a << b << c << first << second << endl;
        count++;
    }                                   // Close files
    ......                                      36
}
```

**Notes**

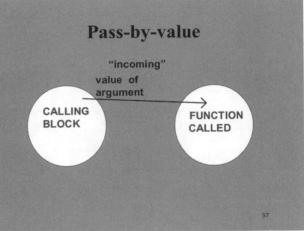

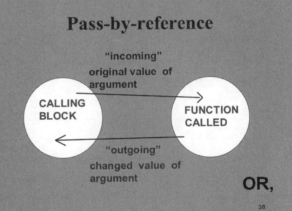

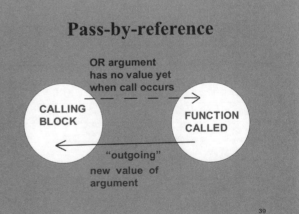

## Data Flow Determines Passing-Mechanism

| Parameter Data Flow | Passing-Mechanism |
|---|---|
| Incoming /* in */ | Pass-by-value |
| Outgoing /* out */ | Pass-by-reference |
| Incoming/outgoing /* inout */ | Pass-by-reference |

40

## Questions

- *Why is a function used for a task?*
  To cut down on the amount of detail in your main program (encapsulation)
- *Can one function call another function?*
  Yes
- *Can a function even call itself?*
  Yes, that is called recursion; it is very useful and requires special care in writing

41

## More Questions

- *Does it make any difference what names you use for parameters?*
  No; just use them in function body
- *Do parameter names and argument names have to be the same?*
  No

42

## Functions are written to specifications

- The specifications state the return type, the parameter types, whether any parameters are "outgoing," and what task the function is to perform with its parameters

- The advantage is that teamwork can occur without knowing what the argument identifiers (names) will be

43

## Write prototype and function definition for

- A void function called GetRating() with one reference parameter of type char

- The function repeatedly prompts the user to enter a character at the keyboard until one of these has been entered: E, G, A, P to represent Excellent, Good, Average, Poor

44

```
void GetRating(char&);        // Prototype

void GetRating(char&   letter)
{
    cout << "Enter employee rating." << endl;
    cout << "Use E, G, A, or P : ";
    cin >> letter;
    while((letter  !=  'E')  &&
          (letter  !=  'G')  &&
          (letter  !=  'A')  &&
          (letter  !=  'P'))
    {
        cout << "Rating invalid.  Enter again: ";
        cin   >> letter;
    }
}
```
45

## A Driver Program

- A driver program is a short `main` program whose only purpose is to test another program

- Write a driver for function `GetRating()`

46

```
#include <iostream>

void  GetRating(char&);      // Prototype

using namespace std;

int main()
{
    char   rating;

    GetRating(rating);       // Call

    cout << "That was rating = "
         << rating << endl;

    return 0;
}
```
47

## An Assertion

An assertion is a truth-valued statement--one that is either true or false (not necessarily in C++ code)

Examples

studentCount > 0

sum is assigned  &&  count > 0

response == 'y' or 'n'

0.0 <= deptSales <= 25000.0

beta == beta @ entry * 2

48

## Preconditions and Postconditions

- A precondition is an assertion describing everything that the function requires to be true at the moment the function is invoked

- A postcondition describes the state at the moment the function finishes executing, providing the precondition is true

- The *caller* is responsible for ensuring the precondition, and the *function code* must ensure the postcondition
  For example . . . 49

## Function with Postconditions

```
void GetRating(/* out */  char&   letter)
// Precondition:  None
// Postcondition: User has been prompted to enter a letter
//     && letter == one of these input values: E,G,A, or P
{
    cout  << "Enter employee rating." << endl;
    cout  << "Use E, G, A, or P : ";
    cin >> letter;
    while((letter != 'E') && (letter != 'G') &&
         (letter != 'A') && (letter != 'P'))
    {
        cout << "Rating invalid. Enter again: ";
        cin   >> letter;
    }
                                                     50
}
```

## Function with Preconditions and Postconditions

```
void  GetRoots( /* in */ float a, /* in */ float b,
               /* in */ float c, /* out */ float& root1,
               /* out */ float& root2)
// Precondition: a, b, and c are assigned
//     && a != 0  &&  b*b - 4*a*c != 0
// Postcondition: root1 and root2 are assigned
//     &&  root1 and root2 are roots of quadratic with
//     coefficients a, b, c
{
    float temp;
    temp = b * b - 4.0 * a * c;
    root1 =(-b + sqrt(temp)) /(2.0 * a);
    root2 =(-b - sqrt(temp)) /(2.0 * a);
    return;
}
                                                     51
```

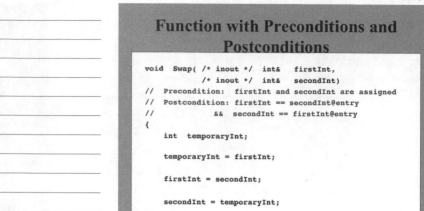

**Notes**

## Chapter 8 Topics

- Local Scope vs. Global Scope of an Identifier
- Detailed Scope Rules to Determine which Variables are Accessible in a Block
- Determining the Lifetime of a Variable
- Writing a Value-Returning Function for a Task
- Some Value-Returning Functions with Prototypes in Header Files cctype and cmath
- Creating and Using a Module Structure Chart
- Stub Testing a Program

## Scope of Identifier

The scope of an identifier (or named constant) is the region of program code in which it is legal to use that identifier for any purpose

# Notes

## Local Scope vs. Global Scope

- The scope of an identifier that is declared *inside* a block (this includes function parameters) extends from the point of declaration to the end of the block

- The scope of an identifier that is declared *outside* of all namespaces, functions, and classes extends from point of declaration to the end of the entire file containing the program code

4

```
const   float   TAX_RATE = 0.05;  // Global constant
float   tipRate;                  // Global variable
void    handle (int,  float);     // Function prototype

using  namespace  std;

int  main ()
{
    int      age;      // age and bill local to this block
    float    bill;
    .                  // a, b, and tax cannot be used here
    .                  // TAX_RATE and tipRate can be used
    handle (age, bill);

    return 0;
}

void  handle (int a,  float b)
{
    float   tax;       // a, b, and tax local to this block
    .                  // age and bill cannot be used here
    .                  // TAX_RATE and tipRate can be used
}
```
5

## Name Precedence Implemented by Compiler Determines Scope

- When an expression refers to an identifier,
  - The compiler first checks the local declarations

  - If the identifier isn't local, the compiler works outward through each level of nesting until it finds an identifier with same name where it stops

- Any identifier with the same name declared at a level further out is never reached

- If compiler reaches global declarations and still can't find the identifier, an error message results

7

## Namespace Scope

- The scope of an identifier declared in a namespace definition extends from the point of declaration to the end of the namespace body, and its scope includes the scope of a using directive specifying that namespace

8

## 3 Ways to Use Namespace Identifiers

- Use a qualified name consisting of the namespace, the scope resolution operator :: and the desired the identifier

```
alpha = std::abs(beta);
```

- Write a using declaration

```
using std::abs;
alpha = abs(beta);
```

- Write a using directive locally or globally

```
using namespace std;
alpha = abs(beta);
```

9

## Name Precedence (or Name Hiding)

- When a function declares a local identifier with the same name as a global identifier, the local identifier takes precedence within that function

10

## Memory Allocation

```
int  someInt;        // For the global variable

int  Square (int n) // For instructions in body
{
    int  result;    // For the local variable
    result  =  n * n;
    return  result;
}
```

11

## No Memory Allocation

```
int  Square (int n);
// Function prototype

extern  int  someInt;
// someInt is defined in another file
// and is thus global to everything in
// this file
```

12

## Lifetime of a Variable

- The lifetime of a variable is the time during program execution in which an identifier actually has memory allocated to it

13

**Notes**

### Lifetime of Local Automatic Variables

- Their storage is created (allocated) when control enters the function

- Local variables are "alive" while function is executing

- Their storage is destroyed (deallocated) when function exits

14

### Lifetime of Global Variables

- Their lifetime is the lifetime of the entire program

- Their memory is allocated when program begins execution

- Their memory is deallocated when the entire program terminates

15

### Automatic vs. Static Variable

| |
|---|
| - Storage for automatic variable is allocated at block entry and deallocated at block exit |

| |
|---|
| - Storage for static variable remains allocated throughout execution of the entire program |

16

## Default Allocation

- Local variables are automatic

- To obtain a static local variable, you must use the reserved word `static` in its declaration

17

## Static and Automatic Local Variables

```
int  popularSquare(int  n)
{
    static int timesCalled = 0;
    // Initialized only once
    int result =  n * n;
    // Initialized each time

    timesCalled  =  timesCalled + 1;
    cout  <<  "Call # "  <<  timesCalled  <<  endl;
    return  result;
}
```

18

## Data Flow Determines Passing-Mechanism

| Parameter Data Flow | Passing-Mechanism |
|---|---|
| Incoming     /* in */ | Pass-by-value |
| Outgoing     /* out */ | Pass-by-reference |
| Incoming/outgoing  /* inout */ | Pass-by-reference |

19

## Notes

### Prototype for `float` Function

AmountDue() is a function with 2 parameters

The first is type char, the other is type int

```
float  AmountDue (char, int);
```

This function calculates and returns the amount due for local phone calls

The char parameter contains either a 'U' or an 'L' indicating Unlimited or Limited service; the int variable contains the number of calls made

Assume Unlimited service is $40.50 per month and limited service is $19.38 for up to 30 calls, and $.09 per additional call

20

```
float AmountDue (char kind, int calls)
// Two parameters
{
    float  result;  // One local variable

    const  float  UNLIM_RATE = 40.50,
                  LIM_RATE = 19.38,
                  EXTRA = .09;
    if (kind =='U')
        result = UNLIM_RATE;

    else if ((kind == 'L') && (calls <= 30))
        result = LIM_RATE;

    else
        result = LIM_RATE + (calls - 30) * EXTRA;

    return result;
}
```

21

```
#include  <iostream>
#include  <fstream>
float AmountDue (char, int);    // Prototype
using  namespace  std;

void  main ()
{
    ifstream  myInfile;
    ofstream  myOutfile;
    int       areaCode, phoneNumber, calls;
    int       count  = 0;
    float     bill;
    char      service;
    . . . . . .                  // Open files
    while (count < 100)
    {
        myInfile >> service >> phoneNumber >> calls;
        bill = AmountDue (service, calls); // Function call
        myOutfile << phoneNumber << bill << endl;
        count++;
    }
    . . . . . .                  // Close files
}
```

22

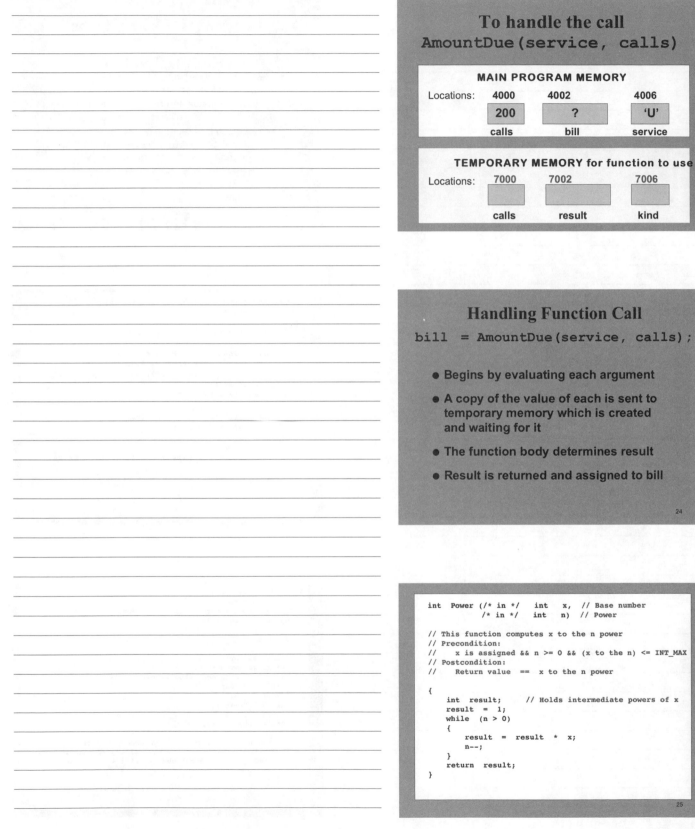

## To handle the call
### AmountDue(service, calls)

**MAIN PROGRAM MEMORY**

| Locations: | **4000** | **4002** | **4006** |
|---|---|---|---|
| | 200 | ? | 'U' |
| | calls | bill | service |

**TEMPORARY MEMORY for function to use**

| Locations: | 7000 | 7002 | 7006 |
|---|---|---|---|
| | | | |
| | calls | result | kind |

23

## Handling Function Call
### bill = AmountDue(service, calls);

- Begins by evaluating each argument
- A copy of the value of each is sent to temporary memory which is created and waiting for it
- The function body determines result
- Result is returned and assigned to bill

24

```
int  Power (/* in */   int   x,  // Base number
            /* in */   int   n)  // Power

// This function computes x to the n power
// Precondition:
//    x is assigned && n >= 0 && (x to the n) <= INT_MAX
// Postcondition:
//    Return value  ==  x to the n power

{
   int  result;     // Holds intermediate powers of x
   result = 1;
   while  (n > 0)
   {
      result = result * x;
      n--;
   }
   return result;
}
```

25

## Syntax Template for Function Definition

```
DataType  FunctionName  ( Parameter List )
{
    Statement
      .
      .
      .
}
```

26

## Using `bool` Type with a Loop

```
   . . .
bool  dataOK;  // Declare Boolean variable
float temperature;
   .   .   .
dataOK = true; // Initialize the Boolean variable
while (dataOK)
{
    .   .   .
    if (temperature  >  5000)
        dataOK = false;
}
```

27

## A Boolean Function

```
bool IsTriangle ( /* in */   float  angle1,
                  /* in */   float  angle2,
                  /* in */   float  angle3)
// Function checks if 3 incoming values add up to
//     180 degrees, forming a valid triangle
// Precondition:
//     angle1, angle2, angle3 are assigned
// Postcondition:
//     Return == true, f sum is within 0.000001 of
//               180.0 degrees
//            == false, otherwise
{
    return (fabs(angle1 + angle2 + angle3 - 180.0)
       <  0.000001);
}
```

28

## Notes

**Some Prototypes in Header File < cctype >**

```
int    isalpha (char  ch);
//  If ch is an alphabet character,
//       Return value == nonzero
//                    == zero, otherwise
int    isdigit (char  ch);
//  If ch is a digit ('0' - '9'),
//       Return value == nonzero
//                    == zero, otherwise
int    islower (char  ch);
//  If ch is a lowercase letter ('a' - 'z'),
//       Return value == nonzero
//                    == zero, otherwise
int    isupper (char  ch);
//  If ch is an uppercase letter ('A' - 'Z'),
//       Return value == nonzero
//                    == zero, otherwise
```
29

**Some Prototypes in Header File < cmath >**

```
double   cos (double  x);
// Return value == trigonometric cosine of angle x
//      in radians
double   exp (double  x);
// Return value == the value e (2.718 . . .) raised to
//      the power x
double   log (double x);
// Return value == natural (base e) logarithm of x

double   log10 (double x);
// Return value == common (base 10) logarithm of x

double   pow (double  x, double y);
// Return value == x raised to the power y
```
30

*What will the function do with your argument(s)?*

**The answer to this question determines whether your function parameter should be value or reference as follows . . .**

31

**Notes**

## Value vs Reference

| If the function-- | Function parameter should be-- |
|---|---|
| only uses its value | /* in */    value parameter |
| assigns it a value | /* out */    reference parameter using & |
| changes its value | /* inout */ reference parameter using & |

*NOTE: I/O stream variables and arrays are exceptions*

32

## Use Void or Value-Returning Functions?

1 If it must return more than one value or modify any of the caller's arguments, do not use a value-returning function

2 If it must perform I/O, do not use a value-returning function

3 If there is only one value returned, and it is Boolean, a value-returning function is appropriate

4 If there is only one value returned, and that value will be used immediately in an expression, a value-returning function is appropriate

5 When in doubt, use a void function; you can recode any value-returning function as a void function by adding an extra outgoing parameter

6 If both void and value-returning are acceptable, use the one you prefer

33

## Use Stubs in Testing a Program

A stub is a dummy function with a very simple body, often just an output statement that this function was reached, and a return value (if any is required) of the correct type

Its name and parameter list is the same as the function that will actually be called by the program being tested

34

## Notes

_____

_____

_____

_____

_____

_____

_____

_____

_____

_____

_____

_____

## Detailed Scope Rules

1 Function names have global scope
2 A function parameter's scope is identical to the scope of a local variable declared in the outermost block of the function body
3 A global variable's (or constant's) scope extends from its declaration to the end of the file, except as noted in rule 5
4 A local variable's (or constant's) scope extends from its declaration to the end of the block in which it is declared, including any nested blocks, except as noted in rule 5
5 An identifier's scope does not include any nested block that contains a locally declared identifier with the same name (local identifiers have name precedence)

6

**Notes**

Chapter 9

Additional Control Structures

Dale/Weems

---

## Chapter 9 Topics

- Switch Statement for Multi-Way Branching
- Do-While Statement for Looping
- For Statement for Looping
- Using break and continue Statements

---

## Switch Statement

The Switch statement is a selection control structure for multi-way branching

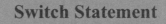
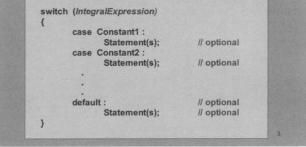

```
switch (IntegralExpression)
{
        case  Constant1 :
                Statement(s);          // optional
        case  Constant2 :
                Statement(s);          // optional
            .
            .
            .
        default :                      // optional
                Statement(s);          // optional
}
```

```
float    weightInPounds  = 165.8;
char     weightUnit;
     . . . // User enters letter for desired weightUnit
switch  (weightUnit)
{
    case 'P' :
    case 'p' :
        cout << weightInPounds  << " pounds " << endl;
        break;
    case 'O' :
    case 'o' :
        cout << 16.0 * weightInPounds  << " ounces " << endl;
        break;
    case 'K' :
    case 'k' :
        cout << weightInPounds / 2.2  << " kilos " << endl;
        break;
    case 'G' :
    case 'g' :
        cout << 454.0 * weightInPounds  << " grams " << endl;
        break;
    default :
        cout << "That unit is not handled! " << endl;
        break;
}                                                        4
```

## Switch Statement

- The value of IntegralExpression (of char, short, int, long or enum type) determines which branch is executed
- Case labels are constant (possibly named) integral expressions
- Several case labels can precede a statement

5

## Control in Switch Statement

- Control branches to the statement following the case label that matches the value of IntegralExpression
- Control proceeds through all remaining statements, including the default, unless redirected with break

- If no case label matches the value of IntegralExpression, control branches to the default label, if present--otherwise control passes to the statement following the entire switch statement

- Forgetting to use break can cause logical errors because after a branch is taken, control proceeds sequentially until either break or the end of the switch statement occurs    6

**Notes**

## Do-While Statement

**Do-While is a looping control structure in which the loop condition is tested *after* each iteration of the loop**

SYNTAX

```
do
{
        Statement

} while (Expression);
```

Loop body statement can be a single statement or a block

7

## Example of Do-While

```
void GetYesOrNo (/* out */  char&  response)
//  Inputs a character from the user
//  Postcondition: response has been input
//              && response == 'y' or 'n'
{
    do
    {
        cin >> response;   // Skips leading whitespace

        if ((response != 'y') && (response != 'n'))
            cout << "Please type  y or n : ";
    } while ((response != 'y') && (response != 'n'));
}
```

8

## Do-While Loop vs. While Loop

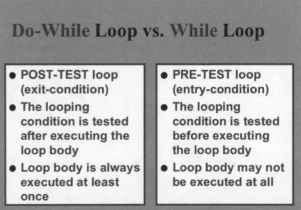

| |
|---|
| ● **POST-TEST loop (exit-condition)** |
| ● **The looping condition is tested after executing the loop body** |
| ● **Loop body is always executed at least once** |

| |
|---|
| ● **PRE-TEST loop (entry-condition)** |
| ● **The looping condition is tested before executing the loop body** |
| ● **Loop body may not be executed at all** |

9

## Notes

### Do-While Loop

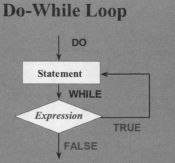

DO

Statement

WHILE

*Expression*

TRUE

FALSE

When the expression is tested and found to be false, the loop is exited and control passes to the statement that follows the Do-while statement   10

### For Loop

SYNTAX

```
for (initialization;  test expression; update)
{
        Zero or more statements to repeat

}
```

11

For loop contains

● An initialization

● An expression to test for continuing

● An update to execute after each iteration of the body

12

## Example of For Loop

```cpp
int   num;

for (num = 1; num <= 3; num++)
{
    cout  <<  num  <<  "Potato"
          <<  endl;
}
```

13

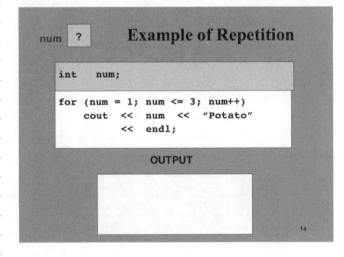

num   ?      **Example of Repetition**

```cpp
int   num;

for (num = 1; num <= 3; num++)
    cout  <<  num  <<  "Potato"
          <<  endl;
```

OUTPUT

14

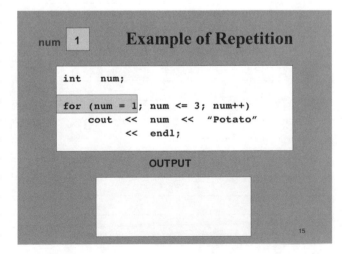

num   1      **Example of Repetition**

```cpp
int   num;

for (num = 1; num <= 3; num++)
    cout  <<  num  <<  "Potato"
          <<  endl;
```

OUTPUT

15

## Notes

Example of Repetition

```
num  1

int    num;
                   true
for(num = 1; num <= 3; num++)

    cout  <<  num  <<  "Potato"
               <<  endl;
           OUTPUT
```

16

Example of Repetition

```
num  1

int    num;

for (num = 1; num <= 3; num++)

    cout  <<  num  <<  "Potato"
               <<  endl;
           OUTPUT

    1Potato
```

17

Example of Repetition

```
num  2

int    num;

for (num = 1; num <= 3; num++)

    cout  <<  num  <<  "Potato"
               <<  endl;
           OUTPUT

    1Potato
```

18

**Notes**

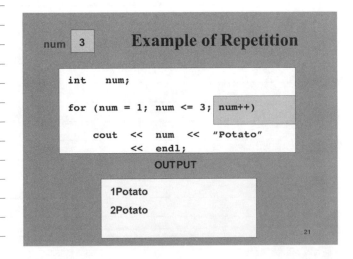

**Example of Repetition**

num `2`

```
int    num;
                true
for(num = 1; num <= 3; num++)

    cout  <<   num  <<  "Potato"
                  <<  endl;
```
OUTPUT

```
1Potato
```

19

**Example of Repetition**

num `2`

```
int   num;

for (num = 1; num <= 3; num++)

    cout  <<   num  <<  "Potato"
                  <<  endl;
```
OUTPUT

```
1Potato
2Potato
```

20

**Example of Repetition**

num `3`

```
int    num;

for (num = 1; num <= 3; num++)

    cout  <<   num  <<  "Potato"
                  <<  endl;
```
OUTPUT

```
1Potato
2Potato
```

21

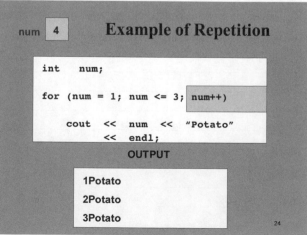

# Notes

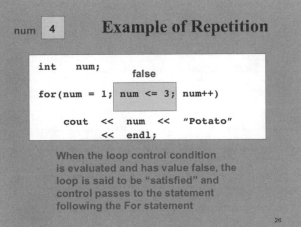

num 4 — **Example of Repetition**

```
int   num;
                 false
for(num = 1; num <= 3; num++)

    cout << num << "Potato"
            << endl;
         OUTPUT
```

```
1Potato
2Potato
3Potato
```

25

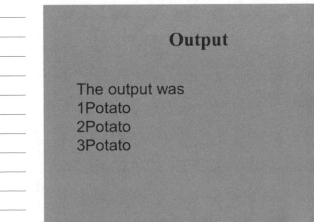

num 4 — **Example of Repetition**

```
int   num;
                 false
for(num = 1; num <= 3; num++)

    cout << num << "Potato"
            << endl;
```

When the loop control condition
is evaluated and has value false, the
loop is said to be "satisfied" and
control passes to the statement
following the For statement

26

## Output

The output was
1Potato
2Potato
3Potato

27

# Notes

### Count-controlled Loop

```
int  count;

for  (count = 4; count > 0; count--)
{
    cout  <<  count  <<  endl;
}

cout   <<  "Done"  <<  endl;
```

OUTPUT:    4
           3
           2
           1
           Done

28

### What is output?

```
int   count;

for (count = 0; count < 10; count++)
{
    cout   <<   "*";
}
```

29

### Answer

```
**********
```

*The 10 asterisks are all on one line.  Why?*

30

## Notes

### What output from this loop?

```
int  count;

for (count = 0;  count < 10;  count++);
{
    cout  <<  "*";
}
```

31

### Answer

- No output from the for loop!  *Why?*
- The semicolon after the () means that the body statement is a null statement
- In general, the body of the For loop is whatever statement *immediately* follows the ()
- That statement can be a single statement, a block, or a null statement
- Actually, the code outputs one * after the loop completes counting to 10

32

### Several Statements in Body Block

```
const  int  MONTHS = 12;
int     count;
float   bill;
float   sum = 0.0;
for (count = 1;  count <= MONTHS;  count++)
{
    cout << "Enter bill: ";
    cin  >> bill;
    sum = sum + bill;
}
cout << "Your total bill is : "  << sum <<  endl;
```

33

## Break Statement

- The Break statement can be used with Switch or any of the 3 looping structures

- It causes an immediate exit from the Switch, While, Do-While, or For statement in which it appears

- If the Break statement is inside nested structures, control exits only the innermost structure containing it

34

## Guidelines for Chooling Looping Statement

- For a simple count-controlled loop, use the For statement
- For an event-controlled loop whose body always executes once, use of Do-While statement
- For an event-controlled loop about which nothing is known, use a While statement
- When in doubt, use a While statement

35

## Continue Statement

- The Continue statement is valid only within loops

- It terminates the current loop iteration, but not the entire loop

- In a For or While, Continue causes the rest of the body of the statement to be skipped; in a For statement, the update is done

- In a Do-While, the exit condition is tested, and if true, the next loop iteration is begun

## Problem

Given a character, a length, and a width, draw a box

For example, given the values '&', 4, and 6, you would display

```
&&&&&&
&&&&&&
&&&&&&
&&&&&&
```

37

## Prototype for Void Function

Call your function  DrawBox () with 3 parameters, the first is type char,  the other 2 are type int.

```
void DrawBox(char,  int,  int);
```

Identifiers may appear in prototypes, but are not necessary

```
void DrawBox(char  letter,  int  num1,
    int  num2);
```

38

```
void DrawBox(char what, int down, int across)
                // 3 parameters
{
    int row, col;      // 2 local variables

    for (row = 0; row < down; row++)
    {
        for (col = 0; col < across; col++)
        {
            cout << what;
        }
        cout << endl;
    }
    return;
}
```

39

## Notes

_____

_____

_____

_____

_____

_____

_____

_____

_____

_____

_____

_____

### The Driver Program

```
#include <iostream>

void DrawBox (char, int, int);    // Prototype

int main ()
{
    char letter = '&';

    DrawBox(letter, 4, 2*3);      // Function call
    DrawBox('V', 9, 3);           // Function call
    return 0;
}
```

40

**Notes**

## Chapter 10

### Simple Data Types: Built-In and User-Defined

Dale/Weems

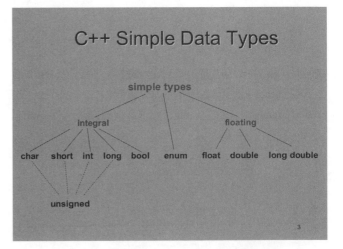

## Chapter 10 Topics

- External and Internal Representations of Data
- Integral and Floating Point Data Types
- Using Combined Assignment Operators
- Prefix and Postfix Forms of Increment and Decrement Operators
- Using Ternary Operator
- Using Type Cast Operator
- Using an Enumeration Type
- Creating and Including User-Written Header Files

## C++ Simple Data Types

simple types

integral — floating

char short int long bool enum float double long double

unsigned

### By definition,

The size of a C++ char value is always 1 byte

**'A'**

exactly one byte of memory space

Sizes of other data type values in C++ are machine-dependent

4

### Using one byte (= 8 bits)

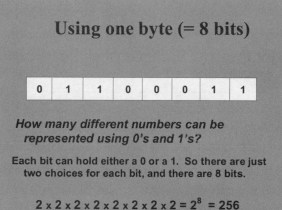

| 0 | 1 | 1 | 0 | 0 | 0 | 1 | 1 |

*How many different numbers can be represented using 0's and 1's?*

Each bit can hold either a 0 or a 1. So there are just two choices for each bit, and there are 8 bits.

$2 \times 2 \times 2 \times 2 \times 2 \times 2 \times 2 \times 2 = 2^8 = 256$

5

### Using two bytes (= 16 bits)

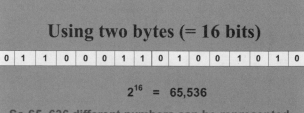

| 0 | 1 | 1 | 0 | 0 | 0 | 1 | 1 | 0 | 1 | 0 | 0 | 1 | 0 | 1 | 0 |

$2^{16} = 65{,}536$

So 65, 636 different numbers can be represented

If we wish to have only one number representing the integer zero, and half of the remaining numbers positive, and half negative, we can obtain the 65,536 numbers in the range -32,768 . . . . 0 . . . . 32,767

6

## Some Integral Types

| Type | Size in Bytes | Minimum Value | Maximum Value |
|------|---------------|---------------|---------------|
| char | 1 | -128 | 127 |
| short | 2 | -32,768 | 32,767 |
| int | 2 | -32,768 | 32,767 |
| long | 4 | -2,147,483,648 | 2,147,483,647 |

NOTE: Values given for one machine; actual sizes are machine-dependent

7

## Data Type `bool`

- Domain contains only 2 values, true and false

- Allowable operation are the logical (!, &&, ||) and relational operations

8

## Operator `sizeof`

`sizeof` A C++ unary operator that yields the size on your machine, in bytes, of its single operand. The operand can be a variable name, or it can be the name of a data type enclosed in parentheses.

```
int  age;
cout  <<  "Size in bytes of variable age is "
      <<  sizeof  age  <<  end;
cout  <<  "Size in bytes of type float is "
      <<  sizeof (float) <<  endl;
```

9

Simple Data Types: Built-In and User-Defined

## The only guarantees made by C++ are . . .

1 = sizeof(char) <= sizeof(short) <= sizeof(int) <= sizeof(long)

1 <= sizeof (bool) <= sizeof (long)

sizeof (float) <= sizeof (double) <= sizeof (long double)

char is at least 8 bits

short is at least 16 bits

long is at least 32 bits

10

## Exponential (Scientific) Notation

2.7E4   means   $2.7 \times 10^{4}$  =

2.7000        =

27000.0

2.7E-4   means   $2.7 \times 10^{-4}$ =

0002.7       =

0.00027

11

## Floating Point Types

| Type | Size in Bytes | Minimum Positive Value | Maximum Positive Value |
|------|---------------|------------------------|------------------------|
| float | 4 | 3.4E-38 | 3.4E+38 |
| double | 8 | 1.7E-308 | 1.7E+308 |
| long double | 10 | 3.4E-4932 | 1.1E+4932 |
| NOTE: Values given for one machine; actual sizes are machine-dependent | | | |

12

## More about Floating Point Types

- Floating point constants in C++ like 94.6 without a suffix are of type double by default

- To obtain another floating point type constant a suffix must be used

  ■ The suffix F or f denotes float type, as in 94.6F

  ■ The suffix L or l denotes long double, as in 94.6L

13

## Header Files
## `climits` and `cfloat`

- Contain constants whose values are the maximum and minimum for your machine
- Such constants are FLT_MAX, FLT_MIN, LONG_MAX, LONG_MIN

```
#include  <climits>
using  namespace  std;
      .
      .
      .
cout  <<  "Maximum long is "  <<  LONG_MAX
      <<  endl;
cout  <<  "Minimum long is "  <<  LONG_MIN
      <<  endl;
```

14

## Combined Assignment Operators

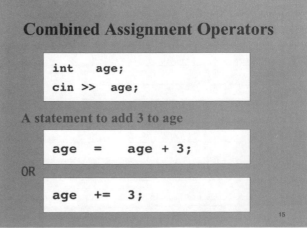

```
int    age;
cin >>  age;
```

A statement to add 3 to age

```
age  =    age + 3;
```

OR

```
age  +=  3;
```

15

**Notes**

A statement to subtract 10 from weight

```
int     weight;
cin >>  weight;
```

```
weight  =   weight - 10;
```

OR

```
weight  -=  10;
```

16

A statement to divide money by 5.0

```
float   money;
cin >>  money;
```

```
money  =  money / 5.0;
```

OR

```
money  /= 5.0;
```

17

A statement to double profits

```
float   profits;
cin >>  profits;
```

```
profits  = profits * 2.0;
```

OR

```
profits  *=  2.0;
```

18

### A statement to raise `cost` 15%

```
float    cost;
cin >>   cost;
cost = cost + cost * 0.15;
```

OR

```
cost = 1.15 * cost;
```

OR

```
cost *= 1.15;
```

19

## *Which form to use?*

● When the increment (or decrement) operator is used in a *"stand alone"* statement to add one (or subtract one) from a variable's value, it can be used in either prefix or postfix form

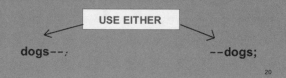

USE EITHER

dogs--;                    --dogs;

20

## BUT...

● when the increment (or decrement) operator is used in a statement with other operators, the prefix and postfix forms can yield *different* results

Let's see how...

21

# Notes

## PREFIX FORM
### "First increment, then use "

```
int  alpha;
int  num;

num = 13;


alpha = ++num * 3;
```

| 13 | |
|----|----|
| num | alpha |

| 14 |
|----|
| num |

| 14 | 42 |
|----|----|
| num | alpha |

22

## POSTFIX FORM
### "Use, then increment"

```
int  alpha;
int  num;

num = 13;


alpha = num++  * 3;
```

| 13 | |
|----|----|
| num | alpha |

| 13 | 39 |
|----|----|
| num | alpha |

| 14 |
|----|
| num |

23

## Type Cast Operator

The C++ cast operator, which comes in two forms, is used to explicitly request a type conversion

```
int      intVar;
float    floatVar  =  104.8;

intVar  =  int(floatVar);   // Functional notation, OR
intVar  =  (int)floatVar;   // Prefix notation uses ()
```

| 104.8 | 104 |
|-------|-----|
| floatVar | intVar |

24

## Ternary (three-operand) Operator
## ? :

SYNTAX

> *Expression1* ? *Expression2* : *Expression3*

MEANING

If *Expression1* is true (nonzero), then the value of the entire expression is *Expression2*. Otherwise, the value of the entire expression is *Expression 3*.

For example . . .    25

## Using Conditional Operator

```
float    Smaller (float  x,  float  y)
// Finds the smaller of two float values
// Precondition: x assigned  &&  y assigned
// Postcondition:Function value  ==   x, if x < y
//                               ==  y, otherwise
{
    float    min;

    min  = (x < y)  ?   x :  y;
    return  min;
}
```
26

## C++ Operator Precedence
## (highest to lowest)

| Operator | Associativity |
|---|---|
| () | Left to right |
| unary: ++  --  !  +  -  (cast)  sizeof | Right to left |
| *   /   % | Left to right |
| +   - | Left to right |
| <   <=   >   >= | Left to right |
| ==  != | Left to right |
| && | Left to right |
| \|\| | Left to right |
| ? : | Right to left |
| =   +=   -=   *=   /= | Right to left |

27

# Notes

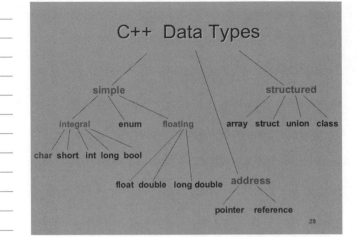

## C++ Data Types

- simple
  - integral
    - char  short  int  long  bool
  - enum
  - floating
    - float  double  long double
- structured
  - array  struct  union  class
- address
  - pointer  reference

28

## ASCII and EBCDIC

- ASCII (pronounced ask-key) and EBCDIC are two character sets commonly used to represent characters internally as one-byte integers

- ASCII is used on most personal computers; EBCDIC is used mainly on IBM mainframes

- The character 'A' is internally stored as integer 65 in ASCII and 193 in EBCDIC

- In both sets, uppercase and lowercase letters are in alphabetical order, allowing character comparisons such as 'A' < 'B', 'a' < 'b'...

- ASCII is a subset of Unicode, a character set that uses two bytes to represent each character

29

### ASCII (Printable) Character Set

| Left Digit(s) \ Right Digit | 0 | 1 | 2 | 3 | 4 | 5 | 6 | 7 | 8 | 9 |
|---|---|---|---|---|---|---|---|---|---|---|
| 3 | | | ! | " | # | $ | % | & | ' | |
| 4 | ( | ) | * | + | , | - | . | / | 0 | 1 |
| 5 | 2 | 3 | 4 | 5 | 6 | 7 | 8 | 9 | : | ; |
| 6 | < | = | > | ? | @ | A | B | C | D | E |
| 7 | F | G | H | I | J | K | L | M | N | O |
| 8 | P | Q | R | S | T | U | V | W | X | Y |
| 9 | Z | [ | \ | ] | ^ | _ | ` | a | b | c |
| 10 | d | e | f | g | h | I | j | k | l | m |
| 11 | n | o | p | q | r | s | t | u | v | w |
| 12 | x | y | z | { | | | } | ~ | | | |

30

## Incrementing char Variables

- Because char variables are stored internally as integers, they can be incremented and compared

EXAMPLE

```
char  ch;
// loop to print out letters A thru Z

for  (ch = 'A';  ch <= 'Z';   ch++)
{
    cout  <<  ch;
}
```

31

## Control Characters

- In addition to the printable characters, character sets also have nonprintable control characters to control the screen, printer, and other hardware
- In C++ programs, control characters are represented by escape sequences formed by a backslash followed by one or more additional characters

32

## Some Escape Sequences

| | |
|---|---|
| \n | Newline (Line feed in ASCII) |
| \t | Horizontal tab |
| \b | Backspace |
| \a | Alert (bell or beep) |
| \\ | Backslash |
| \' | Single quote (apostrophe) |
| \" | Double quote (quotation mark) |
| \0 | Null character (all zero bits) |
| \ddd | Octal equivalent (3 octal digits) |
| \xddd | Hexadecimal equivalent (1 or more hex digits for integer value of character) |

33

**Notes**

## Converting `char` digit to `int`

● The successive digit characters '0' through '9' are represented in ASCII by the successive integers 48 through 57 (the situation is similar in EBCDIC)

● As a result, the following expression converts a char digit value to its corresponding integer value

```
  '2'              ?
  ch             number
```

```
char ch;
int   number;
. . .
number = int (ch - '0')
```
34

## Character Function Prototypes
## in < cctype >

```
int   toupper (int  ch);
// Return value is uppercase equivalent of ch
// If ch is already uppercase, it is not changed
```

```
int   tolower (int  ch);
// Return value is lowercase equivalent of ch
// If ch is already lowercase, it is not changed
```

NOTE:  Although parameter and return type are int, in concept
        these functions operate on character data
35

## Reading a Yes or No User Response

```
String  inputStr;
    :
cout  << "Enter Yes or No";
cin  >> inputStr;
if  (toupper (inputStr [0]) == 'Y')
{// First letter was 'Y' or 'y'
    :
    :
}
else if (toupper (inputStr [0]) == 'N')
{// First letter was 'N' or 'n'
    :
    :
}
else
    PrintErrorMsg ();
```
36

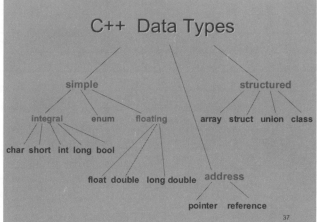

## C++ Data Types

```
                    C++  Data Types
              /                            \
          simple                        structured
        /    |    \                    /    |    |    \
  integral  enum  floating        array struct union class
  /  |  |  |  \
char short int long bool
              float double long double    address
                                          /      \
                                      pointer  reference
                                                        37
```

## typedef statement

- typedef creates an additional name for an already existing data type
- Before bool type became part of ISO-ANSI C++, a Boolean type was simulated this way

```
typedef  int  Boolean;
const  Boolean  true  = 1;
const  Boolean  false  = 0;
        .
        .
Boolean dataOK;
        .
        .
dataOK  =  true;
                                        38
```

## Enumeration Types

- C++ allows creation of a new simple type by listing (enumerating) all the ordered values in the domain of the type

EXAMPLE

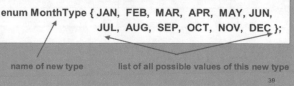

```
enum MonthType { JAN, FEB, MAR, APR, MAY, JUN,
              JUL, AUG, SEP, OCT, NOV, DEC };
```

name of new type          list of all possible values of this new type

39

**Notes**

## enum Type Declaration

```
enum MonthType { JAN, FEB, MAR, APR, MAY, JUN,
                 JUL, AUG, SEP, OCT, NOV, DEC};
```

- The enum declaration creates a new programmer-
  defined type and lists all the possible values of that
  type--any valid C++ identifiers can be used as values

- The listed values are ordered as listed; that is,
  JAN < FEB < MAR < APR , and so on

- You must still declare variables of this type

40

## Declaring enum Type Variables

```
enum  MonthType { JAN,  FEB,  MAR,  APR,  MAY,  JUN,
                  JUL,  AUG,  SEP,  OCT,  NOV,  DEC };

MonthType  thisMonth; // Declares 2 variables
MonthType  lastMonth; // of type MonthType

lastMonth  =  OCT;     // Assigns values
thisMonth  =  NOV;     // to these variables
      .
      .
      .
lastMonth = thisMonth;
thisMonth = DEC;
```

41

## Storage of enum Type Variables

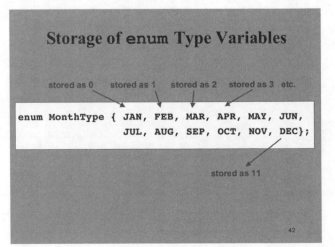

42

## Use Type Cast to Increment enum Type Variables

```
enum MonthType { JAN, FEB, MAR, APR, MAY, JUN,
                 JUL, AUG, SEP, OCT, NOV, DEC};
MonthType  thisMonth;
MonthType  lastMonth;

lastMonth  =  OCT;
thisMonth  =  NOV;
lastMonth = thisMonth;

thisMonth = thisMonth++; // COMPILE ERROR !

thisMonth = MonthType(thisMonth + 1);
// Uses type cast
```

43

## More about enum Type

Enumeration type can be used in a Switch statement for the switch expression and the case labels

Stream I/O (using the insertion << and extraction >> operators) is not defined for enumeration types; functions can be written for this purpos

Comparison of enum type values is defined using the 6 relational operators (< , <= , > , >= , == , !=)

An enum type can be the return type of a value-returning function in C++

44

```
MonthType  thisMonth;

switch (thisMonth) // Using enum type switch expression
{
    case   JAN  :
    case   FEB  :
    case   MAR  :    cout << "Winter quarter";
                        break;
    case   APR  :
    case   MAY  :
    case   JUN  :    cout << "Spring quarter";
                        break;
    case   JUL  :
    case   AUG  :
    case   SEP  :    cout << "Summer quarter";
                        break;
    case   OCT  :
    case   NOV  :
    case   DEC  :    cout << "Fall quarter";
}
```

45

## Using enum type Control Variable with for Loop

```
enum  MonthType { JAN,  FEB,  MAR,  APR,  MAY, JUN,
                  JUL,  AUG,  SEP,  OCT,  NOV,  DEC };

void  WriteOutName (/* in */ MonthType); // Prototype
           .
           .
           .
MonthType  month;

for  (month = JAN; month <= DEC;
        month = MonthType (month + 1))
// Requires use of type cast to increment
{
     WriteOutName (month);
     // Function call to perform output
        :
}                                                  46
```

```
void   WriteOutName ( /* in */ MonthType   month)
// Prints out month name
// Precondition:  month is assigned
// Postcondition: month name has been written out

{ switch (month)
  {
        case JAN : cout << " January ";    break;
        case FEB : cout << " February ";   break;
        case MAR : cout << " March ";      break;
        case APR : cout << " April ";      break;
        case MAY : cout << " May ";        break;
        case JUN : cout << " June ";       break;
        case JUL : cout << " July ";       break;
        case AUG : cout << " August ";     break;
        case SEP : cout << " September ";  break;
        case OCT : cout << " October ";    break;
        case NOV : cout << " November ";   break;
        case DEC : cout << " December ";   break;
  }
}                                                  47
```

## Function with enum Type Return Value

```
enum SchoolType {PRE_SCHOOL, ELEM_SCHOOL,
   MIDDLE_SCHOOL,  HIGH_SCHOOL,  COLLEGE };
      :
SchoolType    GetSchoolData (void)

// Obtains information from keyboard to determine level
// Postcondition: Return value == personal school level
{
     SchoolType  schoolLevel;
     int age;
     int lastGrade;
     cout  << "Enter age :   "; // Prompt for information
     cin  >> age;

                                                   48
```

# Notes

_____

_____

_____

_____

_____

_____

_____

_____

_____

_____

_____

_____

_____

_____

_____

_____

_____

_____

_____

_____

_____

_____

_____

_____

_____

_____

_____

_____

_____

_____

_____

```
if  (age  <   6)
    schoolLevel = PRE_SCHOOL;

else
{
    cout
        << "Enter last grade completed in school: ";
    cin >> lastGrade;
    if  (lastGrade  <  5)
        schoolLevel  =  ELEM_SCHOOL;
    else if  (lastGrade  <  8)
        schoolLevel  =  MIDDLE_SCHOOL;
    else if  (lastGrade  < 12)
        schoolLevel  =  HIGH_SCHOOL;
    else
        schoolLevel  =  COLLEGE;
}
return  schoolLevel;  // Return enum type value
}
```
49

## Multifile C++ Programs

- C++ programs often consist of several different files with extensions such as .h and .cpp

- Related typedef statements, const values, enum type declarations, and similar items are often placed in user-written header files

- By using the #include preprocessor directive the, contents of these header files are inserted into any program file that uses them

50

## Inserting Header Files

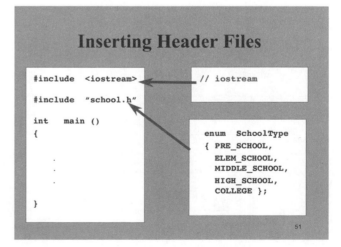

51

## Implicit type coercion occurs . . .

whenever values of different data types are used in:

1. arithmetic and relational expressions

2. assignment operations

3. parameter passage

4. returning a function value with return
   (from a value-returning function)

Two rules apply . . .

52

## Promotion (or widening) in C++

- Promotion is the conversion of a value from a "lower" type to a "higher" type--specifically, for mixed type expressions:

Step 1. Each char, short, bool, or enumeration value is promoted to int; if both operands are now int, the result is an int expression

Step 2. If Step 1 leaves a mixed-type expression, the value of the "lower" operand is promoted to the a value of the "higher" type using the following precedence of types

```
int, unsigned int, long, unsigned long, float, double,
long double
```

For an arithmetic expression, the result is an expression of the "higher" type

For a relational expression, the result is always bool (true or false)

53

## Demotion (or narrowing) . . .

- Demotion is the conversion of a value from a "higher" type to a "lower" type, and may cause loss of information

FOR EXAMPLE,

| 98.6 | 98 |
|------|-----|
| temperature | number |

```
float   temperature  =  98.6;
int     number;
number = temperature;   // Demotion occurs
```

54

# Chapter 11: Structured Types, Data Abstraction, and Classes

## Notes

**Chapter 11**

Structured Types, Data Abstraction and Classes

Dale/Weems

**Chapter 11 Topics**

- Meaning of a Structured Data Type
- Declaring and Using a struct Data Type
- C++ union Data Type
- Meaning of an Abstract Data Type
- Declaring and Using a class Data Type
- Using Separate Specification and Implementation Files
- Invoking class Member Functions in Client Code
- C++ class Constructors

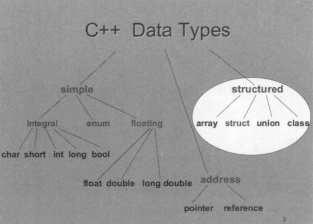

C++ Data Types

simple

integral   enum   floating

char short int long bool

float double long double

structured

array struct union class

address

pointer reference

**Notes**

## Structured Data Type

A **structured** data type is a type in which each value is a collection of component items
- The entire collection has a single name
- Each component can be accessed individually
- Used to bundle together related data of various types for convenient access under the same identifier

For example . . .

4

## thisAnimal

5000

| | |
|---|---|
| .id | 2037581 |
| .name | "giant panda" |
| .genus | "Ailuropoda" |
| .species | "melanoluka" |
| .country | "China" |
| .age | 18 |
| .weight | 234.6 |
| .health | Good |

5

## anotherAnimal

6000

| | |
|---|---|
| .id | 5281003 |
| .name | "llama" |
| .genus | "Lama" |
| .species | "peruana" |
| .country | "Peru" |
| .age | 7 |
| .weight | 278.5 |
| .health | Excellent |

6

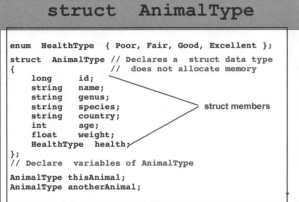

### struct AnimalType

```
enum  HealthType  { Poor, Fair, Good, Excellent };
struct  AnimalType // Declares a  struct data type
{                  //  does not allocate memory
    long      id;
    string    name;
    string    genus;
    string    species;                    struct members
    string    country;
    int       age;
    float     weight;
    HealthType  health;
};
// Declare  variables of AnimalType

AnimalType thisAnimal;
AnimalType anotherAnimal;
```

### struct type Declaration

**SYNTAX**

```
struct  TypeName        // Does not allocate memory
{
    MemberList
};
```

**MemberList SYNTAX**

```
DataType  MemberName;
DataType  MemberName;
   .
   .
   .
```

### struct type Declaration

The struct declaration names a type and names the members of the struct

It does not allocate memory for any variables of that type!

You still need to declare your struct variables

**Notes**

## More about
## `struct` type declarations

**Scope of a struct**
- If the struct type declaration precedes all functions, it will be visible throughout the rest of the file
- If it is placed within a function, only that function can use it

It is common to place struct type declarations in a (.h) header file and #include that file

It is possible for members of *different* struct types to have the same identifiers; also a non-struct variable may have the same identifier as a structure member

10

## Accessing `struct` Members

Dot (period) is the member selection operator

After the struct type declaration, the various members can be used in your program only when they are preceded by a struct variable name and a dot

EXAMPLES

```
thisAnimal.weight
anotherAnimal.country
```

11

## Operations on struct Members

**The type of the member determines the allowable operations**

```
thisAnimal.age  =  18;
thisAnimal.id   =  2037581;
cin >>  thisAnimal.weight;
getline (cin, thisAnimal.species);
thisAnimal.name = "giant panda";
thisAnimal.genus[0] = toupper(thisAnimal.genus[0]);
thisAnimal.age++;
```

12

## Aggregate Operation

An aggregation operation is an operation on a data structure as a whole, as opposed to an operation on an individual component of the data structure

13

## Aggregate struct Operations

- Operations valid on struct type variables are
  - Assignment to another struct variable of the same type
  - Pass as an argument (by value or by reference)
  - Return as value of a function
- I/O, arithmetic, and comparisons of entire struct variables are NOT ALLOWED!

14

## Aggregate struct Operations

```
anotherAnimal = thisAnimal;          // Assignment

WriteOut(thisAnimal);                // Value parameter

ChangeWeightAndAge(thisAnimal);      // Reference parameter

thisAnimal = GetAnimalData();        // Function return value
```

15

```
void WriteOut( /* in */ AnimalType  thisAnimal)
// Prints out values of all members of thisAnimal
// Precondition: all members of thisAnimal are assigned
// Postcondition:all members have been written out
{
    cout << "ID # " << thisAnimal.id
         << thisAnimal.name  << endl;

    cout << thisAnimal.genus << thisAnimal.species
         << endl;

    cout << thisAnimal.country << endl;

    cout << thisAnimal.age << " years " << endl;

    cout << thisAnimal.weight << " lbs. " << endl;

    cout << "General health : ";

    WriteWord (thisAnimal.health);
}
```
16

## Passing a struct Type by Reference

```
void ChangeAge(/* inout */ AnimalType& thisAnimal)

// Adds 1 to age
// Precondition: thisAnimal.age is assigned
// Postcondition:thisAnimal.age ==
//    thisAnimal.age@entry + 1

{

    thisAnimal.age++;

}
```
17

```
AnimalType GetAnimalData ()

// Obtains all information about an animal from keyboard
// Postcondition:
//   Return value == AnimalType members entered at kbd
{
    AnimalType  thisAnimal;
    char response;
    do
    {
    // Have user enter members until they are correct
                         .

                         .

                         .

    }  while (response != 'Y');
    return  thisAnimal;
}
```
18

188                                                                Chapter 11

## Hierarchical Structures

- The type of a struct member can be another struct type

- This is called nested or hierarchical structures

- Hierarchical structures are very useful when there is much detailed information in each record

For example . . .    19

## struct MachineRec

Information about each machine in a shop contains:

an idNumber,

a written description,

the purchase date,

the cost,

and a history (including failure rate, number of days down, and date of last service)

20

```
struct  DateType
{
    int     month;        //  Assume 1 . . 12
    int     day;          //  Assume 1 . . 31
    int     year;         //  Assume 1900 . . 2050
};
struct  StatisticsType
{
    float  failRate;
    DateType lastServiced; //  DateType is a struct type
    int downDays;
};
struct MachineRec
{
    int idNumber;
    string description;
    StatisticsType   history; // StatisticsType is a struct
    DateType  purchaseDate;
    float cost;
};
MachineRec  machine;
                                                          21
```

**Notes**

## struct type variable `machine`

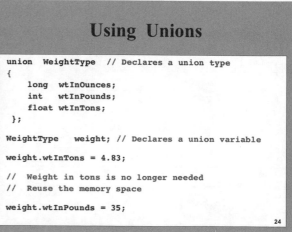

7000

| 5719 | "DRILLING..." | .02 | 1 | 25 | 1999 | 4 | | 3 | 21 | 1995 | 8000.0 |
|------|---------------|-----|---|----|------|---|---|---|----|------|--------|

.month .day .year

.failrate   .lastServiced   .downdays      .month .day .year

.idNumber .description . history                          .purchaseDate   .cost

machine.history.lastServiced.year **has value 1999**

22

## Unions in C++

**DEFINITION**

**A union is a struct that holds only one of its members at a time during program execution.**

**EXAMPLE**

```
union WeightType
{
    long wtInOunces;
    int  wtInPounds;        Only one at a time
    float wtInTons;
};
```
23

## Using Unions

```
union   WeightType  // Declares a union type
{
    long  wtInOunces;
    int   wtInPounds;
    float wtInTons;
};

WeightType   weight; // Declares a union variable

weight.wtInTons = 4.83;

//   Weight in tons is no longer needed
//   Reuse the memory space

weight.wtInPounds = 35;
```
24

## Abstraction

- Abstraction is the separation of the essential qualities of an object from the details of how it works or is composed

  - Focuses on what, not how

  - Is necessary for managing large, complex software projects

25

## Control Abstraction

- Constrol abstraction separates the logical properties of an action from its implementation

  `Search (list, item, length, where, found);`

- The function call depends on the function's specification (description), not its implementation (algorithm)

26

## Data Abstraction

- Data abstraction separates the logical properties of a data type from its implementation

| LOGICAL PROPERTIES | IMPLEMENTATION |
|---|---|
| What are the possible values? | How can this be done in C++? |
| What operations will be needed? | How can data types be used? |

27

## Data Type

set of values
(domain)

allowable operations
on those values

FOR EXAMPLE, data type `int` has

domain

operations

-32768 . . . 32767

+, -, *, /, %, >>, <<

28

## Abstract Data Type (ADT)

- An **abstract data type** is a data type whose properties (domain and operations) are specified (*what*) independently of any particular implementation (*how*)

For example . . .

29

## ADT Specification Example

TYPE
  Time
DOMAIN
  Each Time value is a time in hours, minutes, and seconds.
OPERATIONS
  Set the time
  Print the time
  Increment by one second
  Compare 2 times for equality
  Determine if one time is "less than" another

30

## Another ADT Specification

**TYPE**
  ComplexNumber
**DOMAIN**
  Each value is an ordered pair of real numbers (a, b)
  representing  a + b*i*
**OPERATIONS**
  Initialize the complex number
  Write the complex number
  Add
  Subtract
  Multiply
  Divide
  Determine the absolute value of a complex number

31

## ADT Implementation

● **ADT implementation**
  ■ **Choose a specific data representation for the abstract data using data types that already exist (built-in or programmer-defined)**
  ■ **Write functions for each allowable operation**

32

## Several Possible Representations of ADT Time

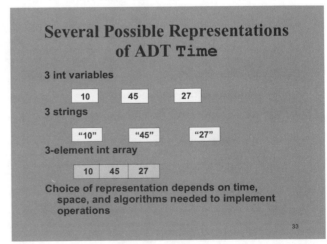

3 int variables

| 10 | | 45 | | 27 |

3 strings

| "10" | | "45" | | "27" |

3-element int array

| 10 | 45 | 27 |

Choice of representation depends on time, space, and algorithms needed to implement operations

33

**Notes**

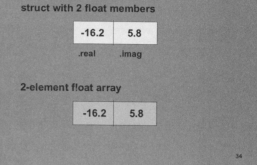

## Some Possible Representations of ADT `ComplexNumber`

**struct with 2 float members**

| -16.2 | 5.8 |
|-------|-----|
| .real | .imag |

**2-element float array**

| -16.2 | 5.8 |
|-------|-----|

34

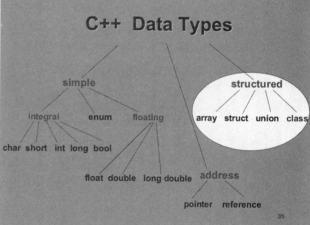

## C++ Data Types

simple

integral    enum    floating

char  short  int  long  bool

float  double  long double    address

pointer    reference

structured

array  struct  union  class

35

## class Time Specification

```
// Specification file (Time.h)
class  Time        // Declares a  class data type
{                  //  does not allocate memory
public :           // Five public function members

    void  Set (int  hours , int  mins , int  secs);
    void  Increment ();
    void  Write ()  const;
    bool  Equal (Time   otherTime)  const;
    bool  LessThan (Time   otherTime)  const;

private :          // Three private data members

    int  hrs;
    int  mins;
    int  secs;
};
```

36

194

## C++ classType

- Facilitates re-use of C++ code for an ADT

- Software that uses the class is called a client

- Variables of the class type are called class objects or class instances

- Client code uses class's public member functions to manipulate class objects

37

## Client Code Using Time

```
#include    "time.h"    // Includes specification of the class
using   namespace   std;

int   main ()
{
    Time    currentTime; // Declares two objects of Time
    Time    endTime;
    bool    done  =  false;

    currentTime.Set (5, 30, 0);
    endTime.Set (18, 30, 0);
    while  (! done)
    {  .   .   .

        currentTime.Increment ();
        if  (currentTime.Equal (endTime))
            done  =  true;
    };
}
```
38

## class type Declaration

The class declaration creates a data type and names the members of the class

It does not allocate memory for any variables of that type!

Client code still needs to declare class variables

39

## Remember ...

- Two kinds of class members:
  data members and function members

- Class members are private by default

- Data members are generally private

- Function members are generally declared public

- Private class members can be accessed only by the class member functions (and friend functions), not by client code

40

## Aggregate class Operations

- Built-in operations valid on class objects are

  Member selection using dot (.) operator ,

  Assignment to another class variable using (=),

  Pass to a function as argument
  (by value or by reference),

  Return as value of a function

- Other operations can be defined as class member functions

41

## Separate Specification and Implementation

```
// Specification file "time.h"
// Specifies the data and function members
class Time
{
public:
          . . .

private:
          . . .
};
```

```
// Implementation file "time.cpp"
// Implements the Time member functions
{
          . . .
}
```

42

## Implementation File for Time

```
// Implementation file "time.cpp"
// Implements the Time member functions.
#include " time.h" // Also must appear in client code
#include  <iostream>
     .   .   .
bool Time::Equal(/* in */  Time otherTime) const
// Postcondition:  Return value == true,
//      if this time equals otherTime,
//      otherwise == false
{
    return ((hrs == otherTime.hrs)
         && (mins == otherTime.mins)
         && (secs  == otherTime.secs));
}
```
43

## Should be familiar ...

- The member selection operator (.) selects either data members or function members

- Header files Iostream and fstream declare the istream, ostream,and ifstream, ofstream I/O classes

- Both cin and cout are class objects and get and ignore are function members

```
cin.get (someChar);
cin.ignore (100, '\n');
```

- These statements declare myInfile as an instance of class ifstream and invoke function member open

```
ifstream  myInfile;
myInfile.open ("mydata.dat");
```
44

## Information Hiding

Information hiding - Class implementation details are hidden from the client's view

Public functions of a class provide the interface between the client code and the class objects

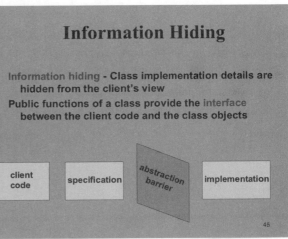

45

## Selection and Resolution

- C++ programs typically use several class types

- Different classes can have member functions with the same identifier, like `Write()`

- Member selection operator is used to determine the object to whom member function Write() is applied
  ```
  currentTime.Write();      // Class Time
  numberZ.Write();          // Class ComplexNumber
  ```

- In the implementation file, the scope resolution operator is used in the heading before the function member's name to specify its class
  ```
  void  Time::Write ()   const
  {           . . .
  }
  ```

46

## Time Class Instance Diagrams

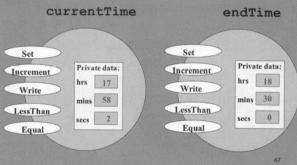

47

## Use of const with Member Functions

- When a member function does not modify the private data members, use const in both the function prototype (in specification file) and the heading of the function definition (in implementation file)

48

## Example Using `const` with a Member Function

```
void Time::Write ()    const

// Postcondition: Time has been output in form
//   HH:MM:SS
{
    if  (hrs < 10)
        cout  << '0';
    cout  << hrs  <<  ':';
    if  (mins < 10)
        cout  << '0';
    cout  << mins  <<  ':';
    if  (secs < 10)
        cout  << '0';
    cout  << secs;
}
```

49

## Separate Compilation and Linking of Files

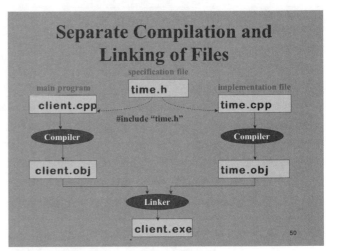

50

## Avoiding Multiple Inclusion of Header Files

- Often several program files use the same header file containing typedef statements, constants, or class type declarations--but, it is a compile-time error to define the same identifier twice within the same namespace

- This preprocessor directive syntax is used to avoid the compilation error that would otherwise occur from multiple uses of #include for the same header file

  ```
  #ifndef Preprocessor_Identifier
  #define Preprocessor_Identifier



  #endif
  ```

51

## Notes

### Example Using Preprocessor Directive #ifndef

```
// time .h
// Specification file

#ifndef  TIME_H
#define  TIME_H

class Time
{
   public:
      . . .

      private:
      . . .
};
#endif
```

For compilation the class declaration in
File time.h will be included only once

```
// time .cpp
// IMPLEMENTATION FILE

#include "time.h"

      . . .
```

```
// client.cpp
// Appointment program

#include "time.h"

int   main (void)
{
      . . .
}
```

52

### Class Constructors

- A class constructor is a member function whose purpose is to initialize the private data members of a class object

- The name of a constructor is always the name of the class, and there is no return type for the constructor

- A class may have several constructors with different parameter lists

- A constructor with no parameters is the default constructor

- A constructor is implicitly invoked when a class object is declared--if there are parameters, their values are listed in parentheses in the declaration  53

### Specification of Time Class Constructors

```
class   Time  // Time.h
{
public :     //   7 function members
    void Set(int hours, int minutes, int seconds);
    void Increment();
    void Write()   const;
    bool Equal(Time otherTime)   const;
    bool LessThan(Time otherTime)   const;

    // Parameterized constructor
    Time (int initHrs, int initMins, int initSecs);
    // Default constructor
    Time();
private :    //   3 data members
    int hrs;
    int mins;
    int secs;
};
```

54

## Implementation of `Time` Default Constructor

```
Time::Time ()
// Default   Constructor
// Postcondition:
//     hrs == 0 && mins == 0 &&   secs == 0
{
    hrs  = 0;
    mins = 0;
    secs = 0;
}
```
55

## Parameterized Constructor

```
Time::Time( /* in */   int   initHrs,
            /* in */   int   initMins,
            /* in */   int   initSecs)
// Constructor
// Precondition:
//     0 <= initHrs <= 23 && 0 <= initMins <= 59
//     0 <= initSecs <= 59
// Postcondition:
//       hrs == initHrs && mins == initMins
//   && secs == initSecs
{
    hrs  = initHrs;
    mins = initMins;
    secs = initSecs;
}
```
56

## Automatic invocation of constructors occurs

```
Time departureTime;  // Default constructor invoked

Time movieTime (19, 30, 0);// Parameterized constructor
```

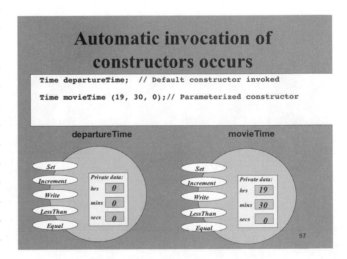

# Chapter 12: Arrays

**Notes**

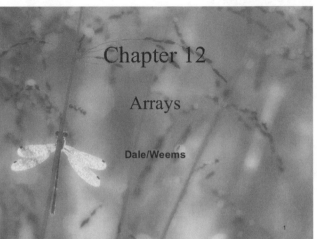

## Chapter 12 Topics

- Declaring and Using a One-Dimensional Array
- Passing an Array as a Function Argument
- Using const in Function Prototypes
- Using an Array of struct or class Objects
- Using an enum Index Type for an Array
- Declaring and Using a Two-Dimensional Array
- Two-Dimensional Arrays as Function Parameters
- Declaring a Multidimensional Array

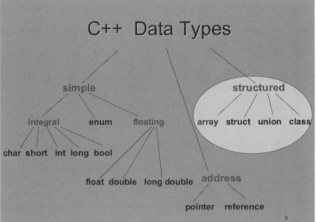

C++ Data Types

simple

integral  enum  floating

char short int long bool

float double long double

structured

array struct union class

address

pointer reference

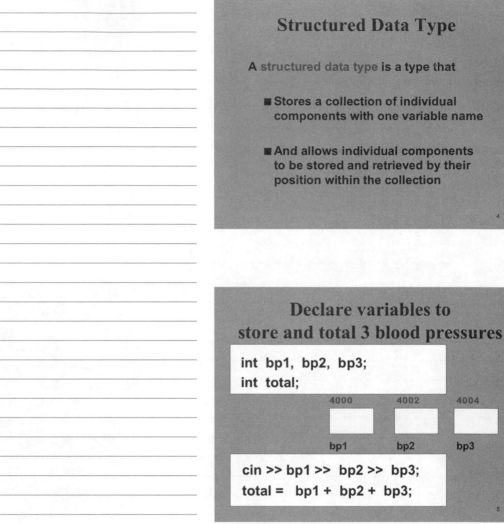

## Structured Data Type

A structured data type is a type that

■ Stores a collection of individual components with one variable name

■ And allows individual components to be stored and retrieved by their position within the collection

## Declare variables to store and total 3 blood pressures

```
int  bp1,  bp2,  bp3;
int  total;
```

```
         4000        4002        4004
```
bp1         bp2         bp3

```
cin >> bp1 >>  bp2 >>  bp3;
total =   bp1 +  bp2 +  bp3;
```

## What if you wanted to store and total 1000 blood pressures?

```
int   bp[1000];
```
// Declares an array of 1000 int values

```
 5000    5002    5004    5006
```
```
                          . . . .
```
bp[0]   bp[1]   bp[2]     . . . .    bp[999]

## One-Dimensional Array Definition

An array is a structured collection of components (called array elements), all of the same data type, given a single name, and stored in adjacent memory locations

The individual components are accessed by using the array name together with an integral valued index in square brackets

The index indicates the position of the component within the collection

## Another Example

- Declare an array called temps which will hold up to 5 individual float values

number of elements in the array

float temps[5];   // Declaration allocates memory

Base Address

| 7000 | 7004 | 7008 | 7012 | 7016 |
|------|------|------|------|------|
| temps[0] | temps[1] | temps[2] | temps[3] | temps[4] |

indexes or subscripts

## Declaration of an Array

- The index is also called the subscript

- In C++, the first array element always has subscript 0, the second array element has subscript 1, etc.

- The base address of an array is its beginning address in memory

SYNTAX

DataType ArrayName[ConstIntExpression];

## Yet Another Example

- Declare an array called name which will hold up to 10 individual char values

number of elements in the array

```
char  name[10];     // Declaration allocates memory
```

Base Address

| 6000 | 6001 | 6002 | 6003 | 6004 | 6005 | 6006 | 6007 | 6008 | 6009 |
|------|------|------|------|------|------|------|------|------|------|
|      |      |      |      |      |      |      |      |      |      |

name[0]  name[1]  name[2]  name[3]  name[4]      . . . . .      name[9]

10

## Assigning Values to Individual Array Elements

```
float temps[5]; int m = 4; // Allocates memory
temps[2] = 98.6;
temps[3] = 101.2;
temps[0] = 99.4;
temps[m] = temps[3] / 2.0;
temps[1] = temps[3] - 1.2;
// What value is assigned?
```

| 7000 | 7004 | 7008 | 7012 | 7016 |
|------|------|------|------|------|
| 99.4 | ? | 98.6 | 101.2 | 50.6 |

temps[0]   temps[1]   temps[2]   temps[3]   temps[4]      11

## *What values are assigned?*

```
float temps[5]; // Allocates memory
int m;

for (m = 0; m < 5; m++)
{
    temps[m] = 100.0 + m * 0.2 ;
}
```

| 7000 | 7004 | 7008 | 7012 | 7016 |
|------|------|------|------|------|
| ? | ? | ? | ? | ? |

temps[0]   temps[1]   temps[2]   temps[3]   temps[4]      12

## Now what values are printed?

```
float temps[5];// Allocates memory
Int m;
. . . . . .
for (m = 4; m >= 0; m--)
{
      cout  <<  temps[m] << endl;
}
```

| 7000 | 7004 | 7008 | 7012 | 7016 |
|------|------|------|------|------|
| 100.0 | 100.2 | 100.4 | 100.6 | 100.8 |

temps[0]  temps[1]  temps[2]  temps[3]  temps[4]   13

## Variable Subscripts

```
float temps[5];// Allocates memory
int m = 3;
. . . . . . .
```

*What is  temps[m + 1] ?*

*What is  temps[m] + 1 ?*

| 7000 | 7004 | 7008 | 7012 | 7016 |
|------|------|------|------|------|
| 100.0 | 100.2 | 100.4 | 100.6 | 100.8 |

temps[0]  temps[1]  temps[2]  temps[3]  temps[4]   14

## A Closer Look at the Compiler

```
float temps[5]; // Allocates memory
```

To the compiler, the value of the identifier temps is
  the base address of the array
We say temps is a pointer (because its value is an
  address);  it "points" to a memory location

| 7000 | 7004 | 7008 | 7012 | 7016 |
|------|------|------|------|------|
| 100.0 | 100.2 | 100.4 | 100.6 | 100.8 |

temps[0]  temps[1]  temps[2]  temps[3]  temps[4]   15

## Initializing in a Declaration

```
int ages[5] ={ 40, 13, 20, 19, 36 };

for (int m = 0; m < 5; m++)
{
    cout  << ages[m];
}
```

| 6000 | 6002 | 6004 | 6006 | 6008 |
|------|------|------|------|------|
| 40 | 13 | 20 | 19 | 36 |
| ages[0] | ages[1] | ages[2] | ages[3] | ages[4] |

16

## Passing Arrays as Arguments

- In C++, arrays are *always* passed by reference

- Whenever an array is passed as an argument, its base address is sent to the called function

17

## In C++, No Aggregate Array Operations

- The only thing you can do with an entire array as a whole (aggregate) is to pass it as an argument to a function

- Exception: aggregate I/O is permitted for C strings (special kinds of char arrays)

18

**Notes**

## Using Arrays as Arguments to Functions

**Generally, functions that work with arrays require 2 items of information**

- The beginning memory address of the array (base address)

- The number of elements to process in the array

19

## Example with Array Parameters

```
#include <iomanip>
#include <iostream>
void  Obtain (int[], int); // Prototypes here
void  FindWarmest (const int[],  int , int&);
void  FindAverage  (const  int[],  int , int&);
void  Print (const  int[], int);

using  namespace  std;

int main ( )
{
    // Array to hold up to 31 temperatures
    int   temp[31
    int   numDays;
    int   average;
    int   hottest;
    int   m;
```
20

## Example continued

```
    cout  <<  "How many daily temperatures? ";
    cin  >>  numDays;

    Obtain(temp, numDays);
    // Call passes value of numDays and address temp
    cout  <<  numDays  <<  " temperatures" << endl;
    Print (temp, numDays);

    FindAverage (temp, numDays, average);
    FindWarmest (temp, numDays, hottest);

    cout  <<  endl  <<  "Average was:  " << average
         <<  endl;
    cout  <<  "Highest was:  "  <<  hottest  << endl;
    return 0;
}
```
21

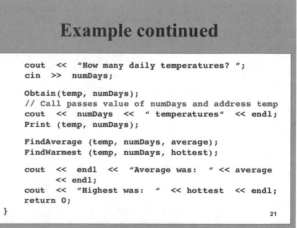

## Notes

### Memory Allocated for Array

```
int temp[31]; // Array to hold up to 31 temperatures
```

Base Address

6000

| 50 | 65 | 70 | 62 | 68 | . . . . . . | | |

temp[0] temp[1] temp[2] temp[3] temp[4]  . . . . .  temp[30]

22

```
void Obtain ( /* out */  int  temp[] ,
              /* in */  int  number )

// User enters number temperatures at keyboard

// Precondition:
//    number is assigned  &&  number > 0
// Postcondition:
//    temp[0 . . number -1]  are assigned
{
    int  m;

    for (m = 0; m < number;  m++)
    {
        cout << "Enter a temperature : ";
        cin >>  temp[m];
    }
}
```
23

```
void Print ( /* in */  const  int  temp[],
             /* in */  int  number )

// Prints number  temperature values to screen
// Precondition:
//    number is assigned  &&  number > 0
//    temp[0 . . number -1] are assigned
// Postcondition:
//    temp[0 . . number -1] printed 5 per line
{
    int  m;
    cout <<   "You entered: ";
    for (m = 0; m < number;  m++)
    {
        if  (m % 5 == 0)
            cout  << endl;
        cout <<  setw(7) << temp[m];
    }
}
```
24

## Use of `const`

- Because the identifier of an array holds the base address of the array, an & is never needed for an array in the parameter list

- Arrays are always passed by reference

- To prevent elements of an array used as an argument from being unintentionally changed by the function, you place `const` in the function prototype and heading

25

## Use of `const` in prototypes

Do not use const with outgoing array because function is supposed to change array values

```
void  Obtain (int[], int);

void  FindWarmest (const int[],  int , int &);

void  FindAverage (const int[],  int , int &);

void  Print (const int[], int);
```

use const with incoming array values to prevent unintentional changes by function

26

```
void FindAverage( /* in */ const int   temp[],
                  /* in */    int   number,
                  /* out */   int &  avg)
// Determines average of temp[0 . . number-1]
// Precondition:
//    number is assigned  &&  number > 0
//    temp[0 . . number -1] are assigned
// Postcondition:
//    avg == average of temp[0 . . number-1]
{
    int  m;
    int  total = 0;
    for (m = 0; m < number;  m++)
    {
        total = total + temp[m];
    }
    avg =
        int (float(total) / float(number) + .5);
}
```
27

## Notes

```
void  FindWarmest ( /* in */ const int temp[],
                    /* in */       int   number,
                    /* out */      int& largest)


// Determines largest of temp[0 . . number-1]
// Precondition:
//    number is assigned  &&  number > 0
//    temp[0 . . number -1] are assigned
// Postcondition:
//    largest== largest value in temp[0 . . number-1]
{
   int  m;
   largest = temp[0]; // Initialize to first element

   for (m = 0; m < number;  m++)
   {
       if (temp[m]  > largest)
           largest  =  temp[m];
   }
}
```
28

## Using arrays for Counters

● **Write a program to count the number of each alphabetic letter in a text file**

| letter | ASCII |
|--------|-------|
| 'A' | 65 |
| 'B' | 66 |
| 'C' | 67 |
| 'D' | 68 |
| . | . |
| . | . |
| . | . |
| 'Z' | 90 |

A:\my.dat

This is my text file.
It contains many
things!
5 + 8 is not 14.
Is it?

29

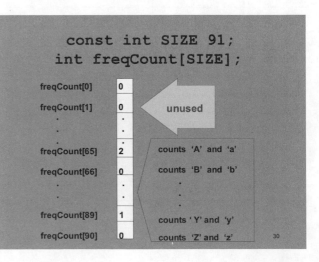

```
const int SIZE 91;
int freqCount[SIZE];
```

| | | |
|---|---|---|
| freqCount[0] | 0 | |
| freqCount[1] | 0 | unused |
| . | . | |
| . | . | |
| . | . | |
| freqCount[65] | 2 | counts 'A' and 'a' |
| freqCount[66] | 0 | counts 'B' and 'b' |
| | . | . |
| | . | . |
| | . | . |
| freqCount[89] | 1 | counts 'Y' and 'y' |
| freqCount[90] | 0 | counts 'Z' and 'z' |

30

## Main Module Pseudocode
### *Level 0*

```
Open dataFile (and verify success)
Zero out freqCount
Read ch from dataFile
WHILE NOT EOF on dataFile
    If ch is alphabetic character
        If ch is lowercase alphabetic
            Change ch to uppercase
        Increment freqCount[ch] by 1
    Read ch from dataFile
Print characters and frequencies
```

31

## Counting Frequency of Alphabetic Characters

```cpp
// Program counts frequency of each alphabetic
//    character in text file.

#include < fstream >
#include < iostream >
#include < cctype >

const int SIZE=91;
void PrintOccurrences(const  int[]); // Prototype

using  namespace  std;
```

32

```cpp
int  main ()
{
    ifstream dataFile;
    int  freqCount[SIZE];
    char ch;
    char index;
    dataFile.open ("my.dat"); // Open
    if  (! dataFile)            // Verify success
    {
        cout  <<  " CAN'T OPEN INPUT FILE ! "
              << endl;
        return  1;
    }
    for ( int  m = 0; m < SIZE;  m++) // Zero array
        freqCount[m]  =  0;
```

33

```
     // Read file one character at a time
     dataFile.get (ch);  // Priming read
     while (dataFile)       // While read successful
     {
         if (isalpha (ch))
         {
             if (islower (ch))
                 ch = toupper (ch);

             freqCount[ch] = freqCount[ch] + 1;
         }
         dataFile. get (ch); // Get next character
     }
     PrintOccurrences (freqCount);
     return 0;
}
```
34

```
 void PrintOccurrences (
     /* in */ const int  freqCount [])
// Prints each alphabet character and its frequency
// Precondition:
//     freqCount['A' . . 'Z'] are assigned
// Postcondition:
//     freqCount['A' . . 'Z'] have been printed
{
    char  index;
    cout << "File contained " << endl;
    cout << "LETTER       OCCURRENCES" << endl;
    for  ( index = 'A' ;  index < = 'Z';  index ++)
    {
        cout << setw(4) << index << setw(10)
             << freqCount[index] << endl;
    }
}
```
35

## More about Array Indexes

- Array indexes can be any integral type including char and enum types
- The index must be within the range 0 through the declared array size minus one
- It is the programmer's responsibility to make sure that an array index does not go out of bounds
- The index value determines which memory location is accessed
- Using an index value outside this range causes the program to access memory locations outside the array

36

**Notes**

## Array with enum Index Type

DECLARATION

```
enum Department { WOMENS,   MENS,   CHILDRENS,
                    LINENS, HOUSEWARES,
   ELECTRONICS };
float   salesAmt[6];
Department which;
```

USE

```
for (which = WOMENS; which <= ELECTRONICS;
  which = Department(which + 1))
     cout  <<  salesAmt[which] << endl;
```
37

## float salesAmt[6];

| | |
|---|---|
| salesAmt[WOMENS] | (i. e. salesAmt[0]) |
| salesAmt[MENS] | (i. e. salesAmt[1]) |
| salesAmt[CHILDRENS] | (i. e. salesAmt[2]) |
| salesAmt[LINENS] | (i. e. salesAmt[3]) |
| salesAmt[HOUSEWARES] | (i. e. salesAmt[4]) |
| salesAmt[ELECTRONICS] | (i. e. salesAmt[5]) |

38

## Parallel Arrays

Parallel arrays are two or more arrays that have the same index range and whose elements contain related information, possibly of different data types

EXAMPLE

```
const int  SIZE 50;
int     idNumber[SIZE];
float   hourlyWage[SIZE];            parallel arrays
```

39

```
const int SIZE 50;
int     idNumber[SIZE];      // Parallel arrays hold
float   hourlyWage[SIZE];    // Related information
```

| idNumber[0] | 4562 | hourlyWage[0] | 9.68 |
| idNumber[1] | 1235 | hourlyWage[1] | 45.75 |
| idNumber[2] | 6278 | hourlyWage[2] | 12.71 |
| . . . | . . . | . . . | . . . |
| idNumber[48] | 8754 | hourlyWage[48] | 67.96 |
| idNumber[49] | 2460 | hourlyWage[49] | 8.97 |

40

## Array of Structures

```
const  int  MAX_SIZE = 500;
enum  HealthType { POOR, FAIR, GOOD, EXCELLENT };
struct  AnimalType  // Declares struct type
{
    long     id;
    string   name;
    string   genus;
    string   species;
    string   country;
    int      age;
    float    weight;
    HealthType health;
};

AnimalType  bronxZoo[MAX_SIZE];   // Declares array
```
41

## AnimalType bronxZoo[MAX_SIZE];

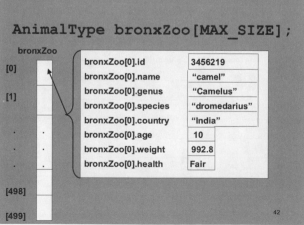

42

## Notes

```
AnimalType bronxZoo[MAX_SIZE];
```

| | .id | .name | .genus | .species | .country | .age | .weight | .health |
|---|---|---|---|---|---|---|---|---|
| bronxZoo[0] | 3456219 | "camel" | "Camelus" | "dromedarius" | "India" | 10 | 992.8 | Fair |
| bronxZoo[1] | | | | | | | | |
| bronxZoo[2] | | | | | | | | |
| bronxZoo[3] | | | | | | | | |
| . | . | | | | | | | |
| . | . | | | | | | | |
| . | . | | | | | | | |
| bronxZoo[498] | | | | | | | | |
| bronxZoo[499] | | | | | | | | |

43

### Add 1 to the age member of each element of the bronxZoo array

```
for (j = 0; j < MAX_SIZE; j++)
    bronxZoo[j].age = bronxZoo[j].age + 1;
```

OR,

```
for (j = 0; j < MAX_SIZE; j++)
    bronxZoo[j].age++;
```

44

### Find total weight of all elements of the bronxZoo array

```
float  total = 0.0;

for (j = 0; j < MAX_SIZE; j++)
    total +=
  bronxZoo[j].weight;
```

45

Arrays

217

# Notes

## Specification of Time

```
class  Time  // "Time.h"
{
public : //  7 function members
    void Set (int hours, int  minutes, int seconds);
    void Increment ();
    void Write ()  const;
    bool  Equal (Time   otherTime)  const;
    bool  LessThan (Time  otherTime)  const;

    Time (int initHrs, int initMins, int initSecs);
    // Constructor
    Time ();
    // Default constructor
private :   // Three data members
  int  hrs;
  int  mins;
  int  secs;
};                                                    46
```

## Time Class Instance Diagram

class   Time

Set

Increment

Write

Equal

LessThan

Time

Time

Private data:

hrs   18

mins   30

secs   0

47

## Array of Class Objects

```
const  int  MAX_SIZE = 50;
// Declare array of class objects
 Time   trainSchedule[MAX_SIZE];
```

The default constructor, if there is any constructor,
is invoked for each element of the array

48

## Two-Dimensional Array

- A two-dimensional array is a collection of components, all of the same type, structured in two dimensions, (referred to as rows and columns)
- Individual components are accessed by a pair of indexes representing the component's position in each dimension

```
DataType ArrayName[ConstIntExpr][ConstIntExpr]...;
```

49

---

EXAMPLE -- Array for monthly high temperatures for all 50 states

```
const int  NUM_STATES  = 50;
const int  NUM_MONTHS = 12;
int  stateHighs[NUM_STATES][NUM_MONTHS];
```

|       | [0] | [1] | [2] | [3] | [4] | [5] | [6] | [7] | [8] | [9] | [10] | [11] |
|-------|-----|-----|-----|-----|-----|-----|-----|-----|-----|-----|------|------|
| [0]   |     |     |     |     |     |     |     |     |     |     |      |      |
| [1]   |     |     |     |     |     |     |     |     |     |     |      |      |
| [2]   |     |     |     |     |     |     |     |     |     |     |      |      |
| ·     | 66  | 64  | 72  | 78  | 85  | 90  | 99  | 105 | 98  | 90  | 88   | 80   |
| ·     |     |     |     |     |     |     |     |     |     |     |      |      |
| [48]  |     |     |     |     |     |     |     |     |     |     |      |      |
| [49]  |     |     |     |     |     |     |     |     |     |     |      |      |

row 2, col 7 might be Arizona's high for August

stateHighs[2][7]

50

---

```
enum  Month { JAN, FEB, MAR, APR, MAY, JUN,
              JUL, AUG, SEP, OCT, NOV, DEC  };
const int  NUM_MONTHS = 12;
const int  NUM_STATES = 50;
int  stateHighs[NUM_STATES][NUM_MONTHS];
```

|       | [JAN] | . | . | . | | | | [AUG] | | . | . | [DEC] |
|-------|-------|---|---|---|---|---|---|-------|---|---|---|-------|
| [0]   |       |   |   |   |   |   |   |       |   |   |   |       |
| [1]   |       |   |   |   |   |   |   |       |   |   |   |       |
| [2]   | 66    | 64| 72| 78| 85| 90| 99| 105   | 98| 90| 88| 80    |
| ·     |       |   |   |   |   |   |   |       |   |   |   |       |
| ·     |       |   |   |   |   |   |   |       |   |   |   |       |
| [48]  |       |   |   |   |   |   |   |       |   |   |   |       |
| [49]  |       |   |   |   |   |   |   |       |   |   |   |       |

row 2, col AUG could be Arizona's high for August

stateHighs[2][AUG]

51

# Notes

```
enum State {  AL, AK, AZ, AR, CA, CO, CT, DE, FL, GA, HI,
    ID, IL, IN, IA, KS, KY, LA, ME, MD, MA, MI, MN, MS, MO,
    MT, NE, NV, NH, NJ, NM, NY, NC, ND, OH, OK, OR, PA, RI,
    SC, SD, TN, TX, UT, VT, VA, WA, WV, WI, WY };
enum Month {  JAN, FEB, MAR, APR, MAY, JUN, JUL,
              AUG, SEP, OCT, NOV, DEC  };
const int NUM_MONTHS = 12;
const int NUM_STATES  = 50;
int stateHighs[NUM_STATES][NUM_MONTHS];
```

|  | [JAN] | | | | | | [AUG] | | | [DEC] | |
|---|---|---|---|---|---|---|---|---|---|---|---|
| [AL] | | | | | | | | | | | |
| [AK] | | | | | | | | | | | |
| [AZ] | 66 | 64 | 72 | 78 | 85 | 90 | 99 | 105 | 98 | 90 | 88 | 80 |

row AZ, col AUG holds Arizona's high for August

stateHighs[AZ][AUG]

[WI]
[WY]

52

---

## Finding the average high temperature for Arizona

```
int  total  = 0;
int  month;        // Without  enum  types
int  average;
for (month = 0; month < NUM_MONTHS; month ++)
    total = total + stateHighs[2][month];
average  = int (total / 12.0  + 0.5);
```

average
**85**

53

---

## Finding the Average High Temperature for Arizona

```
int               total  = 0;
Month month;  // With  enum  types defined
int average;
for (month = JAN; month <= DEC; month = Month(month+1))
     total = total + stateHighs[AZ][month];
average  = int (total / 12.0  + 0.5);
```

average
**85**

54

```
const  int  NUM_STATES   = 50;
const  int  NUM_MONTHS  = 12;
int  stateHighs[NUM_STATES][NUM_MONTHS];
```

rows          columns

STORAGE

● In memory, C++ stores arrays in row order; the first row is followed by the second row, etc.

Base Address

8000          8024          8048

12 highs for state 0    12 highs for state 1    etc.
Alabama                 Alaska
first row               second row

55

## Viewed another way . . .

stateHighs[0][0]
stateHighs[0][1]
stateHighs[0][2]
stateHighs[0][3]
stateHighs[0][4]
stateHighs[0][5]
stateHighs[0][6]
stateHighs[0][7]
stateHighs[0][8]
stateHighs[0][9]
stateHighs[0][10]
stateHighs[0][11]
stateHighs[1][0]
stateHighs[1][1]
stateHighs[1][2]
stateHighs[1][3]

Base Address 8000

To locate an element such as
stateHighs[2][7]
the compiler needs to know
that there are 12 columns
in this two-dimensional array.

At what address will
stateHighs[2][7] be found?

Assume 2 bytes for type int.

56

## Arrays as Parameters

● Just as with a one-dimensional array, when a two- (or higher) dimensional array is passed as an argument, the base address of the caller's array is sent to the function

● The size of all dimensions except the first must be included in the function heading and prototype

● The sizes of those dimensions in the function's parameter list must be exactly the same as those declared for the caller's array

57

Write a function using the two-dimensional stateHighs
array to fill a one-dimensional stateAverages array

```
const  int  NUM_STATES  =  50;
const  int  NUM_MONTHS  =  12;
int  stateHighs[NUM_STATES][NUM_MONTHS];
int  stateAverages[NUM_STATES];
```

|  | [0] | [1] | [2] | [3] | [4] | [5] | [6] | [7] | [8] | [9] | [10] | [11] |
|---|---|---|---|---|---|---|---|---|---|---|---|---|
| [0] |  |  |  |  |  |  |  |  |  |  |  |  |
| [1] |  |  |  |  |  |  |  |  |  |  |  |  |
| [2] | 43 | 42 | 50 | 55 | 60 | 78 | 80 | 85 | 81 | 72 | 63 | 40 |
|  | 66 | 64 | 72 | 78 | 85 | 90 | 99 | 105 | 98 | 90 | 88 | 80 |
| . |  |  |  |  |  |  |  |  |  |  |  |  |
| . |  |  |  |  |  |  |  |  |  |  |  |  |
| . |  |  |  |  |  |  |  |  |  |  |  |  |
| [48] |  |  |  |  |  |  |  |  |  |  |  |  |
| [49] |  |  |  |  |  |  |  |  |  |  |  |  |

Alaska 62
Arizona 85

58

```cpp
void FindAverages(
  /* in */ const int stateHighs[][NUM_MONTHS],
  /* out */       int stateAverages[])

// PRE: stateHighs[0..NUM_STATES][0..NUM_MONTHS]assigned
// POST:stateAverages[0..NUM_STATES] contains rounded
//      rounded high temperature for each state
{
    int  state;
    int  month;
    int  total;
    for (state = 0;  state  <  NUM_STATES;  state++)
    {
        total = 0;
        for (month = 0; month < NUM_MONTHS; month++)
            total += stateHighs[state][month];
        stateAverages[state] = int (total / 12.0 + 0.5);
    }
}
```

59

# Using typedef with Arrays

The typedef statement helps eliminate the chances of size
mismatches between function arguments and
parameters.

**FOR EXAMPLE,**

```cpp
typedef int StateHighs [NUM_STATES][NUM_MONTHS];

typedef int StateAverages [NUM_STATES];


void FindAverages(
  /* in */ const StateHighs stateHighs,
  /* out */       StateAverages stateAverages)
{
}
```

60

**Notes**

## Declaring Multidimensional Arrays

Example of three-dimensional array

```
const NUM_DEPTS = 5;
// mens, womens, childrens, electronics, furniture
const NUM_MONTHS = 12;
const NUM_STORES = 3; // White Marsh,  Owings Mills, Towson

int  monthlySales[NUM_DEPTS][NUM_MONTHS][NUM_STORES];

               rows          columns          sheets
```

OR USING TYPEDEF

```
typedef  int  MonthlySales [NUM_DEPTS][NUM_MONTHS][NUM_STORES];

MonthlySales  monthlySales;                              61
```

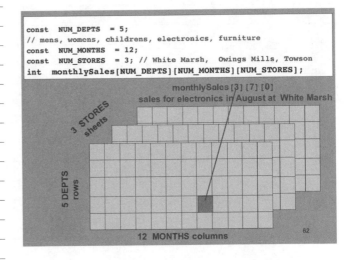

```
const  NUM_DEPTS  = 5;
// mens, womens, childrens, electronics, furniture
const  NUM_MONTHS  = 12;
const  NUM_STORES  = 3; // White Marsh,  Owings Mills, Towson
int  monthlySales[NUM_DEPTS][NUM_MONTHS][NUM_STORES];
```

monthlySales [3] [7] [0]
sales for electronics in August at White Marsh

3 STORES sheets

5 DEPTS rows

12  MONTHS columns                                        62

## Print sales for each month by department

COMBINED SALES FOR January

| DEPT # | DEPT NAME | SALES $ |
|---|---|---|
| 0 | Mens | 8345 |
| 1 | Womens | 9298 |
| 2 | Childrens | 7645 |
| 3 | Electronics | 14567 |
| 4 | Furniture | 21016 |

COMBINED SALES FOR December

| DEPT # | DEPT NAME | SALES $ |
|---|---|---|
| 0 | Mens | 12345 |
| 1 | Womens | 13200 |
| 2 | Childrens | 11176 |
| 3 | Electronics | 22567 |
| 4 | Furniture | 11230 |

63

```
const  NUM_DEPTS  = 5;
// mens, womens, childrens, electronics, furniture
const  NUM_MONTHS  = 12;
const  NUM_STORES  = 3; // White Marsh,  Owings Mills, Towson
int  monthlySales[NUM_DEPTS][NUM_MONTHS][NUM_STORES];
        . . . .
for  (month = 0; month < NUM_MONTHS;  month++)
{
    cout  <<  "COMBINED  SALES  FOR  " ;
    WriteOut(month); // Function call to write the name of month
    cout  <<  "DEPT #        DEPT NAME          SALES $" << endl;

    for  (dept = 0; dept < NUM_DEPTS; dept++)
    {
        totalSales = 0;
        for  (store = 0; store < NUM_STORES; store++)
            totalSales = totalSales +
                         monthlySales[dept][month][store];

        WriteDeptNameAndSales(dept, totalSales);
    }
}                                                          64
```

## Adding a Fourth Dimension . . .

```
const NUM_DEPT = 5;     // mens, womens, childrens …
const NUM_MONTHS = 12;
const NUM_STORES = 3; // White Marsh,  Owings Mills, Towson
const NUM_YEARS  = 2;
int  moreSales[NUM_DEPTS][NUM_MONTHS][NUM_STORES][NUM_YEARS];
```

year 0                    year 1

moreSales[3][7][0][1]
for electronics, August, White Marsh, one year after starting year     65

**Notes**

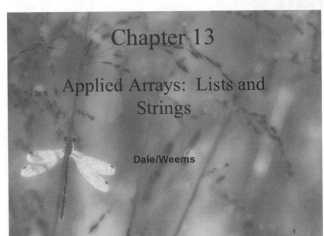

## Chapter 13

### Applied Arrays: Lists and Strings

Dale/Weems

---

## Chapter 13 Topics

- Meaning of a List
- Insertion and Deletion of List Elements
- Selection Sort of List Elements
- Insertion and Deletion using a Sorted List
- Binary Search in a Sorted List
- Order of Magnitude of a Function
- Declaring and Using C Strings
- Using `typedef` with Arrays

---

## *What is a List?*

- A list is a variable-length, linear collection of homogeneous elements

- Linear means that each list element (except the first) has a unique predecessor, and each element (except the last) has a unique successor

## 4 Basic Kinds of ADT Operations

- Constructors -- create a new instance (object) of an ADT

- Transformers -- change the state of one or more of the data values of an instance

- Observers -- allow client to observe the state of one or more of the data values of an instance without changing them

- Iterators -- allow client to access the data values in sequence

4

## ADT List Operations

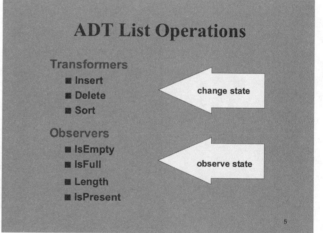

Transformers
- Insert
- Delete
- Sort

change state

Observers
- IsEmpty
- IsFull
- Length
- IsPresent

observe state

5

## ADT List Operations

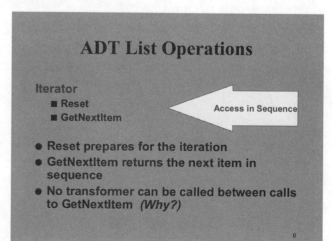

Iterator
- Reset
- GetNextItem

Access in Sequence

- Reset prepares for the iteration
- GetNextItem returns the next item in sequence
- No transformer can be called between calls to GetNextItem *(Why?)*

6

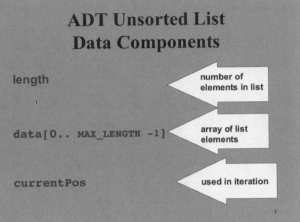

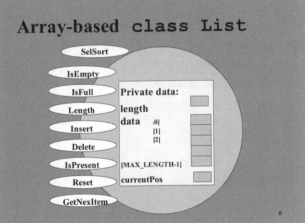

```
// Specification file array-based list ("list.h")
const  int  MAX_LENGTH  =  50;
typedef int    ItemType;

class  List              // Declares a class data type
{
public:                  // Public member functions

    List();              // constructor
    bool IsEmpty () const;
    bool IsFull ()  const;
    int  Length ()  const; // Returns length of list
    void Insert (ItemType  item);
    void Delete (ItemType  item);
    bool IsPresent(ItemType  item)  const;
    void SelSort ();
    void Reset ();
    ItemType GetNextItem ();

private:              // Private data members
    int length;   // Number of values currently stored
    ItemType data[MAX_LENGTH];
    int  CurrentPos;  // Used in iteration
};
                                                9 .
```

## Sorted and Unsorted Lists

| UNSORTED LIST | SORTED LIST |
|---|---|
| Elements are placed into the list in no particular order | List elements are in sorted in some way -- either numerically or alphabetically |

10

```cpp
// Implementation file array-based list ("list.cpp")

#include "list.h"
#include <iostream>

using namespace std;

int  List::Length ()  const
// Post: Return value is length
{
    return  length;
}


bool  List::IsFull ()  const
// Post: Return value is true if length is equal
//   to MAX_LENGTH and false otherwise
{
    return (length == MAX_LENGTH);
}
```

11

```cpp
List::List ()
// Constructor
// Post: length == 0
{
    length = 0;
}

void  List::Insert (/* in */  ItemType  item)
// Pre: length < MAX_LENGTH && item is assigned
// Post: data[length@entry] == item &&
//       length == length@entry + 1
{
    data[length] = item;
    length++;
}
```

12

**Notes**

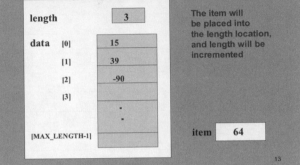

## Before Inserting 64 into an Unsorted List

length     `3`

data   [0]   `15`
       [1]   `39`
       [2]   `-90`
       [3]

[MAX_LENGTH-1]

The item will be placed into the length location, and length will be incremented

item   `64`

13

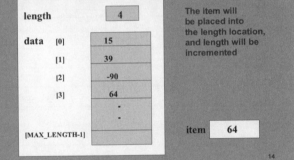

## After Inserting 64 into an Unsorted List

length     `4`

data   [0]   `15`
       [1]   `39`
       [2]   `-90`
       [3]   `64`

[MAX_LENGTH-1]

The item will be placed into the length location, and length will be incremented

item   `64`

14

```
bool  List::IsEmpty ()  const
// Post: Return value is true if length is equal
//   to zero and false otherwise
{
    return (length == 0);
}


bool List::IsPresent( /* in */ ItemType item) const
// Searches the list for item, reporting whether found
// Post: Function value is true, if item is in
//   data[0 . . length-1] and is false otherwise
{
    int index  =  0;
    while (index < length && item != data[index])
        Index++;
    return  (index < length);
}
```
15

## Notes

```
void List::Delete ( /* in */ ItemType item)
// Pre: length > 0  &&  item is assigned
// Post: IF item is in data array at entry
//    First occurrence of item is no longer in array
//       && length == length@entry - 1
//    ELSE
//       length and data array are unchanged
{
   int  index = 0;

   while (index < length  &&  item != data[index])
      index++;
   // IF item found, move last element into
   // item's place
   if (index < length)
   {
      data[index] = data[length - 1];
      length--;
   }
}
```

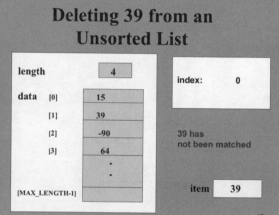

Deleting 39 from an Unsorted List

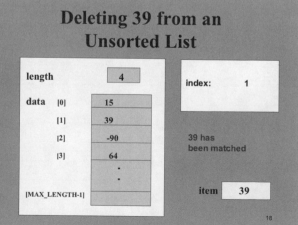

Deleting 39 from an Unsorted List

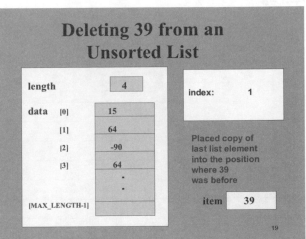

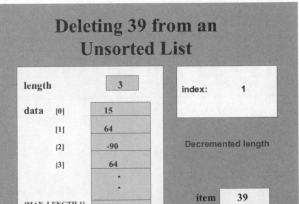

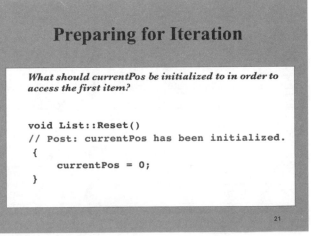

## Iteration Operator

```
ItemType GetNextItem ()
// Pre: No transformer has been executed since last call
// Post:Return value is currentPos@entry
//   Current position has been updated
//   If last item returned, next call returns first item
{
    ItemType item;
    item = data[currentPos];
    if (currentPos == length - 1)
        currentPos = 0;
    else
        currentPos++;
    return item;
}
```

22

## Reset

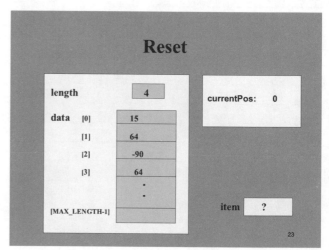

23

## GetNextItem

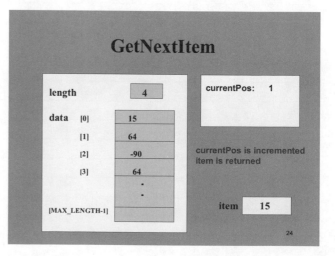

24

## Notes

_____

_____

_____

_____

_____

_____

_____

_____

_____

_____

_____

_____

_____

_____

_____

_____

_____

_____

_____

_____

_____

_____

_____

_____

_____

_____

_____

_____

_____

_____

_____

_____

_____

_____

_____

_____

_____

_____

### Selection Sort Process

Selection sort
- **Examines the entire list to select the smallest element**
- **Places that element where it belongs (with array subscript 0)**
- **Examines the remaining list to select the smallest element from it**
- **Places that element where it belongs (with array subscript 1)**
  .....
- **Examines the last 2 remaining list elements to select the smallest one**
- **Places that element where it belongs in the array**

25

### Selection Sort Algorithm

**FOR passCount going from 0 through length - 2**
    **Find minimum value in data[passCount .. length-1]**
    **Swap minimum value with data[passCount]**

length = 5

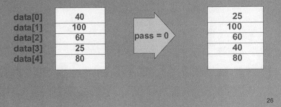

| | pass = 0 | |
|---|---|---|
| data[0] | 40 | 25 |
| data[1] | 100 | 100 |
| data[2] | 60 | 60 |
| data[3] | 25 | 40 |
| data[4] | 80 | 80 |

26

```
void  List::SelSort ()
// Sorts list into ascending order

{
    ItemType temp;
    int passCount;
    int sIndx;
    int minIndx;       // Index of minimum so far
    for (passCount = 0; passCount < length - 1;
        passCount++)
    {
        minIndx = passCount;
        // Find index of smallest value left
        for (sIndx = passCount + 1;
            sIndx <  length; sIndx++)
            if (data[sIndx] = data[minIndx])
                minIndx = sIndx;
        temp = data[minIndx];                // Swap
        data[minIndx] = data[passCount];
        data[passCount] = temp;
    }
}                                              27
```

## Recall: Sorted and Unsorted Lists

| UNSORTED LIST | SORTED LIST |
|---|---|
| Elements are placed into the list in no particular order | List elements are ordered in some way -- either numerically or alphabetically |

28

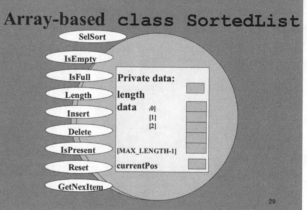

## Array-based class SortedList

- SelSort
- IsEmpty
- IsFull
- Length
- Insert
- Delete
- IsPresent
- Reset
- GetNexItem

Private data:
length
data [0]
     [1]
     [2]

[MAX_LENGTH-1]

currentPos

29

```
// Specification file sorted list ("slist.h")
const int MAX_LENGTH = 50;
typedef int    ItemType;

class SortedList        // Declares a class data type
{
public:                 // Public member functions

    List();             // constructor
    bool IsEmpty () const;
    bool IsFull () const;
    int  Length ()  const; // Returns length of list
    void Insert (ItemType  item);
    void Delete (ItemType  item);
    bool IsPresent(ItemType  item)  const;
    void SelSort ();
    void Reset ();
    ItemType GetNextItem ();

private:                // Private data members
    int length;     // Number of values currently stored
    ItemType data[MAX_LENGTH];
    int  CurrentPos;  // Used in iteration
};
```
30

## Member Functions

*Which member function specifications and implementations must change to ensure that any instance of the SortedList ADT remains sorted at all times?*

■ Insert

■ Delete

31

## Insert Algorithm for SortedList ADT

● **Create space** for the new item by shifting down all the larger list elements

● Put the new item in the list

● Increment length

32

## Implementing `SortedList` Member Function `Insert`

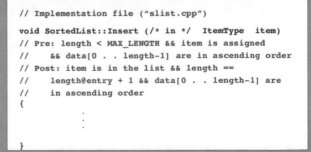

```
// Implementation file ("slist.cpp")

void SortedList::Insert (/* in */  ItemType  item)
// Pre: length < MAX_LENGTH && item is assigned
//    && data[0 . . length-1] are in ascending order
// Post: item is in the list && length ==
//    length@entry + 1 && data[0 . . length-1] are
//    in ascending order
{
           .
           .
           .

}
```

33

```
void  SortedList::Insert (ItemType   item)
{
    int index;
    // Find proper location for new element
    index  =  length - 1;
    // Starting at bottom of array shift down
    //  values larger than item to make room for
    //  new item

    while (index >= 0  &&  item < data[index] )
    {
        data[index + 1]  =  data[index];
        index--;
    }
    // Insert item into array
    data[index] = item;
    length++;
}
                                                    34
```

## Delete Algorithm for SortedList ADT

- Find the position of the element to be deleted from the sorted list

- Eliminate space occupied by the item being deleted by shifting up all the larger list elements

- Decrement length

35

## Implementing SortedList Member Function Delete

```
void  SortedList::Delete (/* in */  ItemType   item)
//  Deletes item from list, if it is there
//  Pre: 0 < length <= INT_MAX/2 && item is assigned
//      && data[0 . . length-1] are in ascending order
// Post: IF item is in data array at entry
//      First occurrence of item is no longer in array
//      && length == length@entry-1
//      && data[0 . . Length-1] are in ascending order
//      ELSE
//      length and data array are unchanged
{
        .
        .
}                                                   36
```

```
void SortedList::Delete (/* in */  ItemType  item)
{
    bool found;      // true, if item is found
    int  position;  // Position of item, if found
    int  index;
    // Find location of element to be deleted

    BinSearch (item, found, position);
    if (found)
    {
     // Shift elements that follow in sorted list

        for (index = position; index < length + 1;
            index++)
            data[index ] = data[index  + 1];
        length--;
    }
}
```

## Improving Member Function
## IsPresent

Recall that with the unsorted List ADT
we examined each list element beginning
with data[0], until we either found a
match with item or we had examined all
the elements in the unsorted List

*How can the searching algorithm be
improved for SortedList ADT?*

## Searching for 55 in a
## SortedList

length           4

data    [0]      15
        [1]      39
        [2]      64
        [3]      90
                  .
                  .
[MAX_LENGTH-1]

A sequential search
for 55 can stop
when 64 has been
examined.

item    55

## Binary Search in SortedList

- Examines the element in the middle of the array
  - Is it the sought item? If so, stop searching
  - Is the middle element too small? Then start looking in second half of array
  - Is the middle element too large? Then begin looking in first half of the array
- Repeat the process in the half of the data that should be examined next

- Stop when item is found or when there is nowhere else to look

40

```
void  SortedList::BinSearch (ItemType  item,   bool&  found,
  int&  position)
//  Searches sorted list for item, returning position of item,
//  if item was found
{
    int middle;
    int first  =  0;
    int last   = length - 1;
    found = false;
    while (last >= first  &&   !found)
    {  middle = (first + last)/2; // Index of middle element

        if (item  <  data[middle])
            last = middle - 1;      // Look in first half next
        else if (item  >  data[middle])
            first = middle + 1;     // Look in second half next
        else
            found = true;           // Item  has been found
    }
    if  (found)
      position = middle;
}
```

41

## Trace of Binary Search

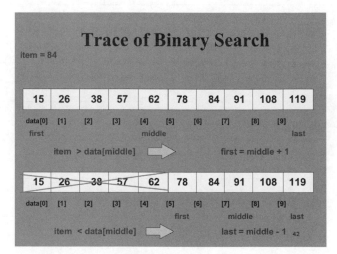

42

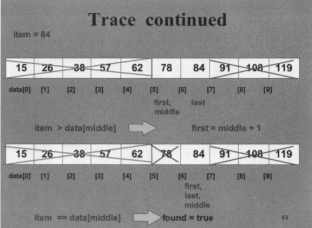

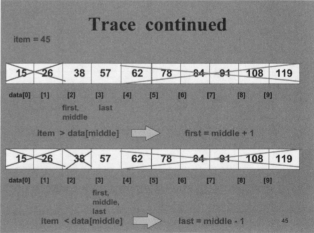

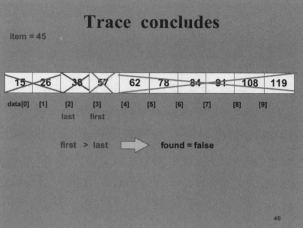

## Trace concludes

item = 45

| 15 | 26 | 38 | 57 | 62 | 78 | 84 | 91 | 108 | 119 |
|----|----|----|----|----|----|----|----|-----|-----|
| data[0] | [1] | [2] | [3] | [4] | [5] | [6] | [7] | [8] | [9] |

last    first

first > last  ⟹  found = false

46

## Still More Efficient `IsPresent`

```
bool  SortedList::IsPresent
   (/* in */  ItemType  item)  const
// Searches list for item, reporting whether found
// Pre: length <= INT_MAX/2 && item is assigned
//    && data[0 . . length-1] are in ascending order
// Post: Return value == true, if item is in
//    data[0 . . length-1] == false, otherwise
{
    bool found;
    int  position;

    BinSearch (item, found, position);

    return  found;
}
```
47

## Comparison of Sequential and Binary Searches

| | Average Number of Iterations to Find *item* | |
|---|---|---|
| **Length** | **Sequential Search** | **Binary Search** |
| 10 | 5.5 | 2.9 |
| 100 | 50.5 | 5.8 |
| 1,000 | 500.5 | 9.0 |
| 10,000 | 5000.5 | 12.4 |

48

## Order of Magnitude of a Function

The order of magnitude, or Big-O notation, of an expression describes the complexity of an algorithm according to the highest order of N that appears in its complexity expression

49

## Names of Orders of Magnitude

| | |
|---|---|
| $O(1)$ | constant time |
| $O(\log_2 N)$ | logarithmic time |
| $O(N)$ | linear time |
| $O(N^2)$ | quadratic time |
| $O(N^3)$ | cubic time |

50

| N | $\log_2 N$ | $N*\log_2 N$ | $N^2$ |
|---|---|---|---|
| 1 | 0 | 0 | 1 |
| 2 | 1 | 2 | 4 |
| 4 | 2 | 8 | 16 |
| 8 | 3 | 24 | 64 |
| 16 | 4 | 64 | 256 |
| 32 | 5 | 160 | 1024 |
| 64 | 6 | 384 | 4096 |
| 128 | 7 | 896 | 16,384 |

51

**Notes**

## Big-O Comparison of List Operations

| OPERATION | UnsortedList | SortedList |
|---|---|---|
| IsPresent | O(N) | O(N)   sequential search<br>$O(\log_2 N)$   binary search |
| Insert | O(1) | O(N) |
| Delete | O(N) | O(N) |
| SelSort | $O(N^2)$ | |

52

## In Addition . . .

To the string class from the standard library accessed by #include <string>

C++ also has another library of string functions for C strings that can be accessed by #include <cstring>

53

## What is a C String?

A C string is a char array terminated by the null character '\0' (with ASCII value 0)

A C string variable can be initialized in its declaration in two equivalent ways.

```
char message[8] = { 'H', 'e', 'l',
   'l', 'o', '\0' };

char  message[8]  =  "Hello";
```

| 'H' | 'e' | 'l' | 'l' | 'o' | '\0' | | |
|---|---|---|---|---|---|---|---|
| message[0] | [1] | [2] | [3] | [4] | [5] | [6] | [7] |

54

## `char` vs. C string

'A'   has data type `char`
and is stored in 1 byte

5000

| 'A' |
|-----|

"A"   is a C string of 2 characters
and is stored in 2 bytes

6000   6001

| 'A' | '\0' |
|-----|------|

55

## Recall that . . .

```
char message[8];
// Declaration allocates memory
```

To the compiler, the value of the identifier **message**
is the base address of the array.  We say **message** is
a pointer (because its value is an address).  It
"points" to a memory location.

6000

| 'H' | 'e' | 'l' | 'l' | 'o' | '\0' | | |
|-----|-----|-----|-----|-----|------|-|-|
| message[0] | [1] | [2] | [3] | [4] | [5] | [6] | [7] |

56

## Aggregate C String I/O in C++

I/O of an entire C string is possible using
the array identifier with no subscripts
and no looping.

EXAMPLE

```
char  message[8];
cin >> message;
cout << message;
```

However . . .

57

## Extraction operator >>

When using the extraction operator (>>) to read input characters into a string variable, the following things happen

● The >> operator skips any leading whitespace characters such as blanks and newlines

● It then reads successive characters into the array and stops at the first trailing whitespace character (which is not consumed, but remains waiting in the input stream)

● The >> operator adds the null character to the end of the string

58

## Example Using >>

```
char   name[5];
cin  >>  name;     total number of elements in the array
```

Suppose input stream looks like this:
  □□J o e□

7000

| 'J' | 'o' | 'e' | '\0' | |
|-----|-----|-----|------|---|

name[0]  name[1]  name[2]  name[3]  name[4]

null character is added              59

## Function get()

● Because the extraction operator stops reading at the first trailing whitespace, >> cannot be used to input a string with blanks in it

● If your string's declared size is not large enough to hold the input characters and add the '\0', the extraction operator stores characters into memory beyond the end of the array

● Use get function with two parameters to overcome these obstacles

EXAMPLE

```
char  message[8];
cin.get (message, 8);
// Inputs at most 7 characters plus '\0'
```

## inFileStream.get (str, count + 1)

- **get** does not skip leading whitespace **characters such as blanks and newlines**

- **get** reads successive characters (including blanks) into the array, and stops when it either has read count characters, or it reaches the newline character '\n', whichever comes first

- **get** appends the null character **to str**

- If newline is reached, it is not consumed **by get**, but remains waiting in the input stream

61

## Function `ignore ()`

- **ignore** can be used to consume any remaining characters up to and including the newline '\n' left in the input stream by **get**

```
cin.get(string1, 81);
// Inputs at most 80 characters
cin.ignore(30, '\n');
// Skips at most 30 characters
//  but stops if '\n' is read
cin.get(string2, 81);
```

62

## Another Example Using `get ()`

```
char   ch;
char   fullName[31];
char   address[31];
cout << "Enter your full name: ";
cin.get (fullName, 31);
cin.get (ch);   // To consume the newline
cout << "Enter your address: ";
cin.get (address, 31);
```

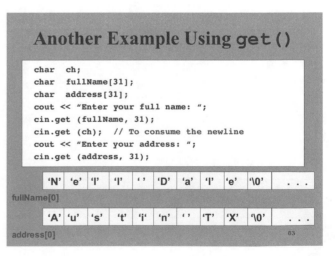

| 'N' | 'e' | 'l' | 'l' | ' ' | 'D' | 'a' | 'l' | 'e' | '\0' | . . . |

fullName[0]

| 'A' | 'u' | 's' | 't' | 'i' | 'n' | ' ' | 'T' | 'X' | '\0' | . . . |

address[0]

63

## Notes

### String Function Prototypes in <cstring >

```
int  strlen (char str[]);
// FCTNVAL   == integer length of string str (not including '\0')


int  strcmp (char str1[], char str2[]);
// FCTNVAL   == negative, if str1 precedes str2 lexicographically
//            == positive, if str1 follows str2 lexicographically
//            == 0, if str1 and str2 characters same through '\0'


char * strcpy (char toStr[],  char fromStr[]);
// FCTNVAL   == base address of toStr (usually ignored)
// POSTCONDITION:   characters in string fromStr are copied to
//                  string toStr, up to and including '\0',
//                  overwriting contents of string toStr
```
64

```
# include   <cstring >
   .
   .
   .
 char author[21];
 int  length;

 cin.get (author, 21);
 length = strlen (author);
 // What is the value of length ?
```

5000

| 'C' | 'h' | 'i' | 'p' | ' ' | 'W' | 'e' | 'e' | 'm' | 's' | '\0' | . . . |

author[0]

65

```
char  myName[21] = "Huang";   // What is output?
char  yourName[21];

cout << "Enter your last name: ";
cin.get (yourName, 21);

if (strcmp (myName, yourName) == 0)
    cout  << "We have the same name! ";
else if (strcmp (myName, yourName) < 0)
    cout  << myName  << " comes before "
          << yourName;
else if  (strcmp (myName, yourName) > 0)
    cout  << yourName  << "comes before "
          << myName;
```

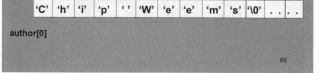

| 'H' | 'u' | 'a' | 'n' | 'g' | '\0' | | | | | . . . |

myName[0]

| 'H' | 'e' | 'a' | 'd' | 'i' | 'n' | 'g' | 't' | 'o' | 'n' | '\0' | . . . |

yourName[0]

66

# Notes

```
char  myName[21] = "Huang";
char  yourName[21];

if (myName  ==  yourName)
// Compares addresses only!
//   That is, 4000 and 6000 here.
//   == does not compare contents!
{

}
```

4000

| 'H' | 'u' | 'a' | 'n' | 'g' | '\0' | | | | | . . . |

myName[0]

6000

| 'H' | 'e' | 'a' | 'd' | 'i' | 'n' | 'g' | 't' | 'o' | 'n' | '\0' | . . . |

yourName[0]

67

```
char  myName[21] = "Huang";
char  yourName[21];

cin.get (yourName, 21);
yourName  =  myName;
                        What happens?
```

4000

| 'H' | 'u' | 'a' | 'n' | 'g' | '\0' | | | | | . . . |

myName[0]

6000

| 'H' | 'e' | 'a' | 'd' | 'i' | 'n' | 'g' | 't' | 'o' | 'n' | '\0' | . . . |

yourName[0]

68

```
char  myName[21]  = "Huang";
char  yourName[21];

cin.get (yourName, 21);
strcpy (yourName, myName);
      What happens?
```

4000

| 'H' | 'u' | 'a' | 'n' | 'g' | '\0' | | | | | . . . |

myName[0]

6000    'u'        'n'    'g'    '\0'

| 'H' | 'e' | 'a' | 'd' | 'i' | 'n' | 'g' | 't' | 'o' | 'n' | '\0' | . . . |

yourName[0]

69

## Notes

_____

_____

_____

_____

_____

_____

_____

_____

_____

_____

_____

## Using `typedef` with Arrays

```
typedef char String20[21];
// Names String20 as an array type

String20    myName;   // These declarations allocate
String20    yourName; // memory for three  variables
bool isSeniorCitizen;
```

5000

6000

7000

70

**Notes**

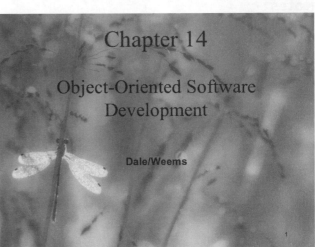

## Chapter 14 Topics

- Structured Programming vs. Object-Oriented Programming
- Using Inheritance to Create a New C++ `class` Type
- Using Composition (Containment) to Create a New C++ `class` Type
- Static vs. Dynamic Binding of Operations to Objects
- Virtual Member Functions

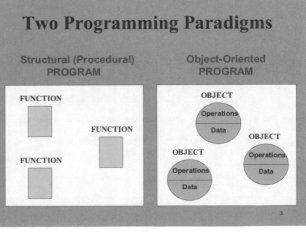

**Notes**

---

### Object-Oriented Programming Language Features

1. Data abstraction

2. Inheritance of properties

3. Dynamic binding of operations to objects

4

---

### OOP Terms          C++ Equivalents

| OOP Terms | C++ Equivalents |
|-----------|-----------------|
| Object | Class object or class instance |
| Instance variable | Private data member |
| Method | Public member function |
| Message passing | Function call ( to a public member function) |

5

---

### What is an object?

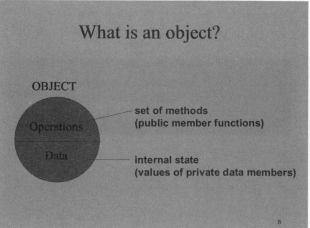

OBJECT

Operations ──── set of methods (public member functions)

Data ──── internal state (values of private data members)

6

---

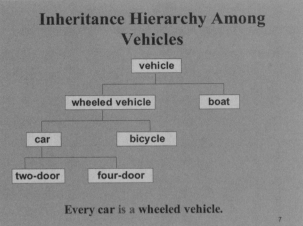

## Inheritance Hierarchy Among Vehicles

vehicle
- wheeled vehicle
  - car
    - two-door
    - four-door
  - bicycle
- boat

**Every car is a wheeled vehicle.**

7

## Inheritance

- Inheritance is a mechanism by which one class acquires (inherits) the properties (both data and operations) of another class

- The class being inherited from is the Base Class (Superclass)

- The class that inherits is the Derived Class (Subclass)

- The derived class is specialized by adding properties specific to it

8

## class Time Specification

```
// Specification file ("time.h")
class  Time
{
public:
    void Set ( int hours, int minutes, int seconds);
    void Increment ();
    void Write ()  const;
    Time ( int initHrs, int initMins, int initSecs);
    // Constructor
    Time ();          // Default constructor
private:
    int hrs;
    int mins;
    int secs;
};
```
9

**Notes**

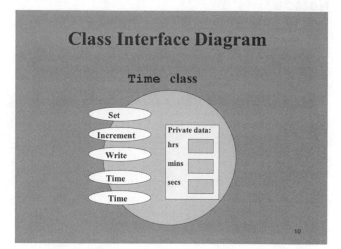

## Class Interface Diagram

Time class

Set
Increment
Write
Time
Time

Private data:
hrs
mins
secs

10

## Using Inheritance to Add Features

```
// Specification file ("exttime.h")
#include   "time.h"
enum ZoneType{EST, CST, MST, PST, EDT, CDT, MDT, PDT};

class ExtTime : public Time // Time is the base class
{
public:
    void Set(int hours, int minutes, int seconds,
            ZoneType  timeZone);
    void Write ()  const;
    ExtTime ( int  initHrs,  int  initMins,
            int  initSecs, ZoneType  initZone);
    ExtTime ();
private:
    ZoneType  zone; // Additional data member
};
```
11

## class ExtTime:public Time

● Says class Time is a public base class of the derived class ExtTime

● As a result, all public members of Time (except constructors) are also public members of ExtTime

● In this example, new constructors are provided, new data member zone is added, and member functions Set and Write are overridden

12

**Notes**

### Class Interface Diagram
#### ExtTime class

### Client Code Using ExtTime

```
#include "exttime.h"
      .
      .
ExtTime  thisTime ( 8, 35, 0, PST);
ExtTime  thatTime; // Default constructor called

thatTime.Write(); // Outputs 00:00:00  EST
cout << endl;

thatTime.Set (16, 49, 23, CDT);
thatTime.Write(); // Outputs 16:49:23  CDT
cout << endl;

thisTime.Increment ();
thisTime.Increment ();
thisTime.Write (); // Outputs 08:35:02  PST
cout << endl;
```

### Constructor Rules for Derived Classes

- At run time, the base class constructor is implicitly called first, before the body of the derived class's constructor executes

- If the base class constructor requires parameters, they must be passed by the derived class's constructor

**Notes**

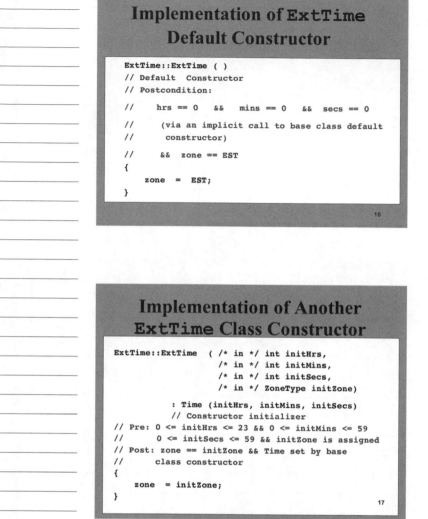

### Implementation of `ExtTime` Default Constructor

```
ExtTime::ExtTime ( )
// Default Constructor
// Postcondition:
//     hrs == 0   &&   mins == 0   &&   secs == 0
//     (via an implicit call to base class default
//     constructor)
//     && zone == EST
{
    zone = EST;
}
```

16

### Implementation of Another `ExtTime` Class Constructor

```
ExtTime::ExtTime   ( /* in */ int initHrs,
                     /* in */ int initMins,
                     /* in */ int initSecs,
                     /* in */ ZoneType initZone)

          : Time (initHrs, initMins, initSecs)
          // Constructor initializer
// Pre: 0 <= initHrs <= 23 && 0 <= initMins <= 59
//      0 <= initSecs <= 59 && initZone is assigned
// Post: zone == initZone && Time set by base
//      class constructor
{
    zone = initZone;
}
```

17

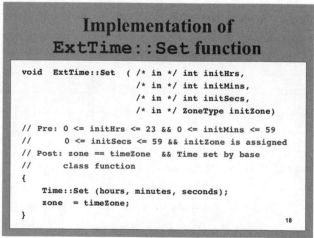

### Implementation of `ExtTime::Set` function

```
void  ExtTime::Set  ( /* in */ int initHrs,
                      /* in */ int initMins,
                      /* in */ int initSecs,
                      /* in */ ZoneType initZone)

// Pre: 0 <= initHrs <= 23 && 0 <= initMins <= 59
//      0 <= initSecs <= 59 && initZone is assigned
// Post: zone == timeZone  && Time set by base
//      class function
{
    Time::Set (hours, minutes, seconds);
    zone = timeZone;
}
```

18

**Notes**

## Implementation of ExtTime::Write Function

```
void ExtTime::Write ( )  const

//  Postcondition:
//      Time has been output in form HH:MM:SS  ZZZ
//      where  ZZZ is the time zone abbreviation
{
    static string zoneString[8] = { "EST", "CST",
        MST", "PST", "EDT", "CDT", "MDT", "PDT" };
    Time::Write ();
    cout  <<  ' ' <<  zoneString[zone];
}
```

19

## Responsibilities

- Responsibilities are operations implemented as C++ functions
- Action responsibilities are operations that perform an action
- Knowledge responsibilities are operations that return the state of private data variables

20

## What responsibilities are Missing?

The Time class needs
  int Hours()
  int Minutes()
  int Seconds()
The ExtTime class needs
  ZoneType zone()

21

## Composition (or Containment)

● Composition (containment) is a mechanism by which the internal data (the state) of one class includes an object of another class

22

## An Entry Object

```
#include "Time.h"
#include "Name.h"
#include <string>
class Entry
{
public:
    string NameStr() const;
    // Returns a string made up of first name and last name
    string TimeStr() const;
    // Returns a string made up of hour, colon, minutes
    Entry();
    // Default constructor
    Entry(......)
    // Parameterized constructor

private:
    Name name;
    Time time;
}
```

## Order in Which Constructors are Executed

Given a class X,

● if X is a derived class its base class constructor is executed first

● next, constructors for member objects (if any) are executed (using their own default constructors if none is specified)

● finally, the body of X's constructor is executed

24

**Notes**

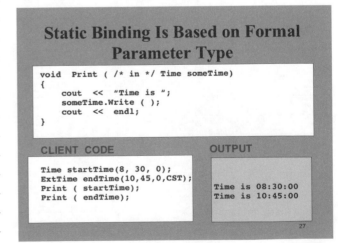

### In C++ . . .

When the type of a formal parameter is a parent class, the argument used can be

- the same type as the formal parameter or,
- any descendant class type

25

### Static Binding

- Static binding is the compile-time determination of which function to call for a particular object based on the type of the formal parameter(s)

- When pass-by-value is used, static binding occurs

26

### Static Binding Is Based on Formal Parameter Type

```
void  Print ( /* in */ Time someTime)
{
    cout << "Time is ";
    someTime.Write ( );
    cout << endl;
}
```

CLIENT CODE

```
Time startTime(8, 30, 0);
ExtTime endTime(10,45,0,CST);
Print ( startTime);
Print ( endTime);
```

OUTPUT

```
Time is 08:30:00
Time is 10:45:00
```

27

## Dynamic Binding

- Dynamic binding is the run-time determination of which function to call for a particular object of a descendant class based on the type of the argument

- Feclaring a member function to be virtual instructs the compiler to generate code that guarantees dynamic binding

28

## Virtual Member Function

```
// Specification file ( "time.h")
class   Time
{
public:

    . . .

    virtual void Write () const;
    // Forces dynamic binding
    . . .

private:

    int   hrs;
    int   mins;
    int   secs;
};
```

## Dynamic binding requires pass-by-reference

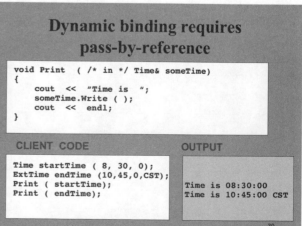

```
void Print  ( /* in */ Time& someTime)
{
    cout  << "Time is  ";
    someTime.Write ( );
    cout  << endl;
}
```

| CLIENT CODE | OUTPUT |
| --- | --- |
| Time startTime ( 8, 30, 0);<br>ExtTime endTime (10,45,0,CST);<br>Print ( startTime);<br>Print ( endTime); | Time is 08:30:00<br>Time is 10:45:00 CST |

30

## Using virtual functions in C++

- Dynamic binding requires pass-by-reference when passing a class object to a function
- In the declaration for a virtual function, the word virtual appears only in the base class
- If a base class declares a virtual function, it must implement that function, even if the body is empty
- A derived class is not required to re-implement a virtual function; if it does not, the base class version is used

31

## Slicing Problem

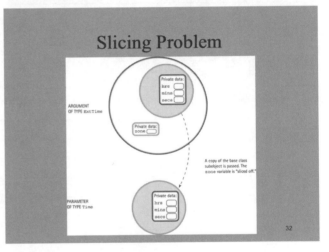

ARGUMENT
OF TYPE ExtTime

Private data:
hrs
mins
secs

Private data:
zone

A copy of the base class subobject is passed. The zone variable is "sliced off."

PARAMETER
OF TYPE Time

Private data:
hrs
mins
secs

32

## Object-Oriented Design

- Identify the Objects and Operations
- Determine the relationship among objects
- Design and Implement the driver

33

## Implementation of the Design

- Choose a suitable data representation
  - Built-in data type
  - Existing ADT
  - Create a new ADT
- Create algorithms for the abstract operations
  - Top-down design is often the best technique to create algorithms for the function tasks

34

## Case Study

- Beginning of the Appointment Calendar Program
- Class Entry composed of a Name class and a Time class
- Current Time class represents active time (seconds with Increment)
- Need a static Time class for time in the appointment calendar
  - *Is inheritance appropriate?*

35

## Notes

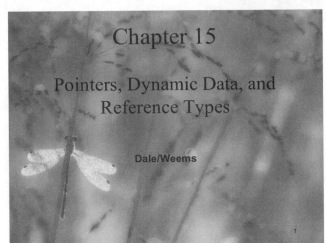

**Chapter 15**

Pointers, Dynamic Data, and Reference Types

Dale/Weems

---

**Chapter 15 Topics**

- Using the Address-Of Operator &
- Declaring and Using Pointer Variables
- Using the Indirection (Dereference) Operator *
- The NULL Pointer
- Using C++ Operators new and delete
- Meaning of an Inaccessible Object
- Meaning of a Dangling Pointer
- Use of a Class Destructor
- Shallow Copy vs. Deep Copy of Class Objects
- Use of a Copy Constructor

---

**Recall that . . .**

char str [ 8 ];

str is the base address of the array. We say str is a pointer because its value is an address. It is a pointer constant because the value of str itself cannot be changed by assignment. It "points" to the memory location of a char.

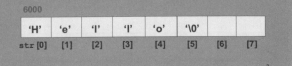

6000

| 'H' | 'e' | 'l' | 'l' | 'o' | '\0' | | |
|-----|-----|-----|-----|-----|------|---|---|
| str [0] | [1] | [2] | [3] | [4] | [5] | [6] | [7] |

## Notes

---

### Addresses in Memory

- When a variable is declared, enough memory to hold a value of that type is allocated for it at an unused memory location. This is the address of the variable

```
int      x;
float    number;
char     ch;
```

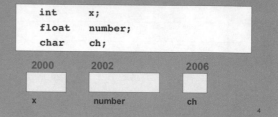

| 2000 | 2002 | 2006 |
|------|------|------|
| x | number | ch |

4

---

### Obtaining Memory Addresses

- the address of a non-array variable can be obtained by using the address-of operator &

```
int      x;
float    number;
char     ch;

cout << "Address of x is " << &x << endl;

cout << "Address of number is " << &number << endl;

cout << "Address of ch is " << &ch << endl;
```

5

---

### What is a pointer variable?

- A pointer variable is a variable whose value is the address of a location in memory

- To declare a pointer variable, you specify the type of value that the pointer will point to, for example

```
int*     ptr; // ptr will hold the address of an int

char*    q;   // q will hold the address of a char
```

6

# Notes

### Using a Pointer Variable

```
int   x;
x = 12;

int*  ptr;
ptr = &x;
```

2000
12
x

3000
2000
ptr

NOTE:  Because ptr holds the address of x,
we say that ptr "points to" x

7

### Unary operator * is the indirection (deference) operator

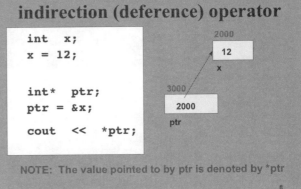

```
int   x;
x = 12;

int*  ptr;
ptr = &x;

cout  <<  *ptr;
```

2000
12
x

3000
2000
ptr

NOTE:  The value pointed to by ptr is denoted by *ptr

8

### Using the Dereference Operator

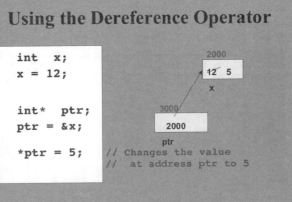

```
int   x;
x = 12;

int*  ptr;
ptr = &x;

*ptr = 5;
```
// Changes the value
// at address ptr to 5

2000
12  5
x

3000
2000
ptr

9

## Notes

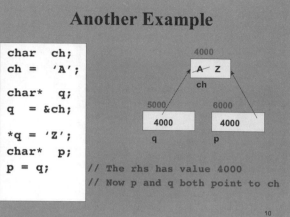

**Another Example**

```
char   ch;
ch =   'A';

char*  q;
q  = &ch;

*q = 'Z';
char*  p;
p = q;          // The rhs has value 4000
                // Now p and q both point to ch
```

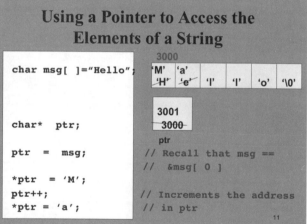

**Using a Pointer to Access the Elements of a String**

```
char msg[ ]="Hello";




char*  ptr;

ptr  =  msg;

*ptr  = 'M';
ptr++;
*ptr = 'a';
```

```
// Recall that msg ==
//   &msg[ 0 ]

// Increments the address
// in ptr
```

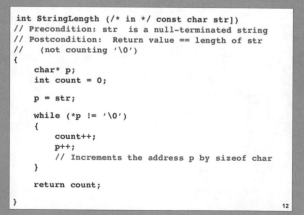

```
int StringLength (/* in */ const char str])
// Precondition: str  is a null-terminated string
// Postcondition:  Return value == length of str
//   (not counting '\0')
{
    char* p;
    int count = 0;

    p = str;

    while (*p != '\0')
    {
        count++;
        p++;
        // Increments the address p by sizeof char
    }

    return count;
}
```

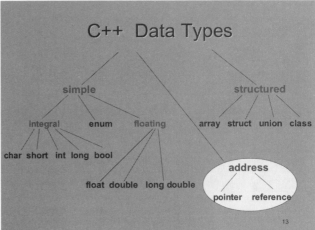

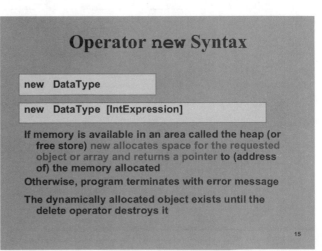

## The NULL Pointer

NULL is a pointer constant 0, defined in header file cstddef, that means that the pointer points to nothing

- It is an error to dereference a pointer whose value is NULL
- Such an error may cause your program to crash, or behave erratically

```
while (ptr != NULL)
{
  . . . // Ok to use *ptr here
}
```

16

## 3 Kinds of Program Data

- Static data: memory allocation exists throughout execution of program
  `static long currentSeed;`

- Automatic data: automatically created at function entry, resides in activation frame of the function, and is destroyed when returning from function

- Dynamic data: explicitly allocated and deallocated during program execution by C++ instructions written by programmer using operators new and delete

17

## Allocation of Memory

| STATIC ALLOCATION | DYNAMIC ALLOCATION |
|---|---|
| Static allocation is the allocation of memory space at compile time | Dynamic allocation is the allocation of memory space at run time by using operator new |

18

# Notes

_____

_____

_____

_____

_____

_____

_____

_____

_____

_____

_____

_____

_____

_____

_____

_____

_____

_____

_____

_____

_____

_____

_____

_____

_____

_____

_____

_____

_____

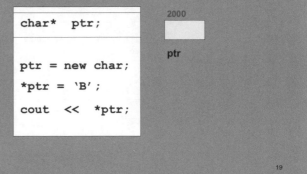

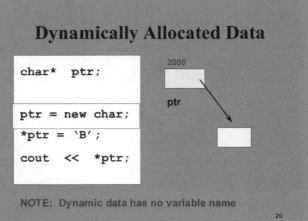

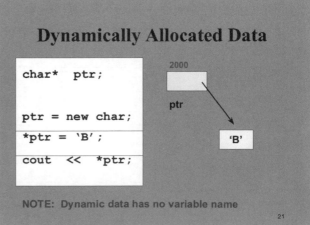

**Notes**

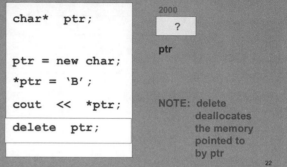

### Dynamically Allocated Data

```
char*  ptr;

ptr = new char;
*ptr = 'B';
cout  <<  *ptr;
delete  ptr;
```

2000
? 
ptr

NOTE: delete
      deallocates
      the memory
      pointed to
      by ptr

22

### Using Operator delete

- Operator delete returns memory to the free store, which was previously allocated at run-time by operator new

- The object or array currently pointed to by the pointer is deallocated, and the pointer is considered unassigned

23

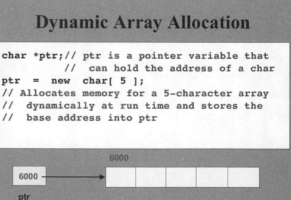

### Dynamic Array Allocation

```
char *ptr;// ptr is a pointer variable that
          //  can hold the address of a char
ptr  =  new  char[ 5 ];
// Allocates memory for a 5-character array
//  dynamically at run time and stores the
//  base address into ptr
```

6000

6000 ⟶ [ ][ ][ ][ ][ ]

ptr

24

## Dynamic Array Allocation

```
char  *ptr;

ptr  =  new  char[ 5 ];

strcpy(ptr, "Bye");

ptr[ 1 ] = 'u';
// A pointer can be subscripted
cout  << ptr[ 2];
```

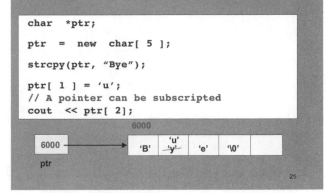

## Operator delete Syntax

delete   Pointer

delete []   Pointer

If the value of the pointer is NULL there is no effect

Otherwise, the object or array currently pointed to by Pointer is deallocated, and the value of Pointer is undefined

The memory is returned to the free store

Square brackets are used with delete to deallocate a dynamically allocated array

## Dynamic Array Deallocation

```
char *ptr;
ptr = new char[ 5 ];
strcpy(ptr, "Bye");
ptr[ 1 ] = 'u';
delete  ptr;
// Deallocates array pointed to by ptr
// ptr itself is not deallocated
// The value of ptr is undefined
```

?

ptr

**Notes**

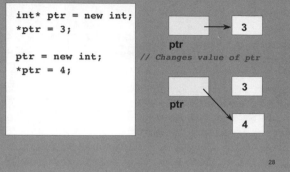

## What happens here?

```
int* ptr = new int;
*ptr = 3;

ptr = new int;
*ptr = 4;
```

ptr → 3

ptr

// Changes value of ptr

ptr

3

ptr

4

28

## Inaccessible Object

An inaccessible object is an unnamed object created by operator new that a programmer has left without a pointer to it.

```
int* ptr = new int;
*ptr = 8;
int* ptr2 = new int;
*ptr2 = -5;
```

ptr → 8

ptr

ptr2 → -5

ptr2

*How else can an object become inaccessible?*

29

## Making an Object Inaccessible

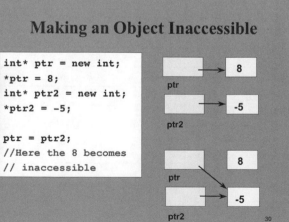

```
int* ptr = new int;
*ptr = 8;
int* ptr2 = new int;
*ptr2 = -5;

ptr = ptr2;
//Here the 8 becomes
// inaccessible
```

ptr → 8

ptr

ptr2 → -5

ptr2

ptr

8

ptr2 → -5

30

## Notes

### Memory Leak

A memory leak is the loss of available memory space that occurs when dynamic data is allocated but never deallocated

31

### A Dangling Pointer

- A dangling pointer is a pointer that points to dynamic memory that has been deallocated

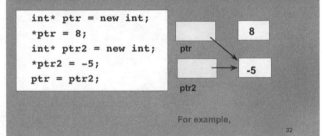

```
int* ptr = new int;
*ptr = 8;
int* ptr2 = new int;
*ptr2 = -5;
ptr = ptr2;
```

For example,

32

### Leaving a Dangling Pointer

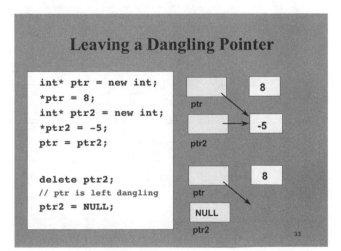

```
int* ptr = new int;
*ptr = 8;
int* ptr2 = new int;
*ptr2 = -5;
ptr = ptr2;

delete ptr2;
// ptr is left dangling
ptr2 = NULL;
```

33

# Notes

```
// Specification file ("dynarray.h")
// Safe integer array class allows run-time specification
// of size, prevents indexes from going out of bounds,
// allows aggregate array copying and initialization

class DynArray
{
public:
    DynArray(/* in */  int arrSize);
        // Constructor
        // PRE:  arrSize is assigned
        // POST: IF arrSize >= 1 && enough memory THEN
        //          Array of size arrSize is created with
        //          all elements == 0  ELSE error message

    DynArray(const DynArray& otherArr);
        // Copy constructor
        // POST: this DynArray is a deep copy of otherArr
        // Is implicitly called for initialization
```
34

```
// Specification file  continued

    ~DynArray();
        // Destructor
        // POST: Memory for dynamic array deallocated

    int  ValueAt (/* in */ int i)  const;
        // PRE:  i is assigned
        // POST: IF 0 <= i < size of this array THEN
        //          FCTVAL == value of array element at index i
        //          ELSE error message

    void  Store (/* in */ int val,  /* in */ int i)
        // PRE:  val and i are assigned
        // POST: IF 0 <= i < size of this array THEN
        //          val is stored in array element i
        //          ELSE error message
```
35

```
// Specification file  continued
    void  CopyFrom (/* in */ DynArray otherArr);
        // POST:  IF enough memory THEN
        //            new array created (as deep copy)
        //            with size and contents
        //            same as otherArr
        //            ELSE error message.

private:
    int*  arr;
    int   size;
};
```
36

Chapter 15

# Notes

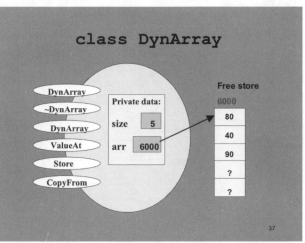

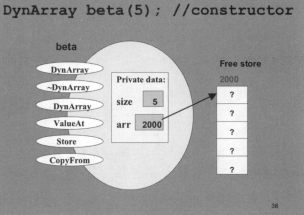

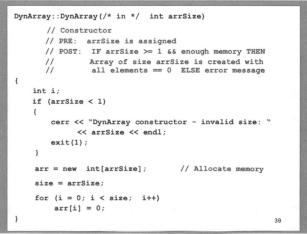

# Notes

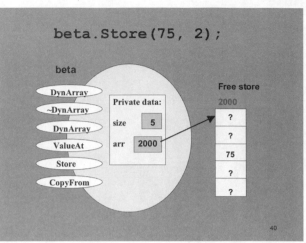

```
beta.Store(75, 2);
```

```
void  DynArray::Store (/* in */ int val,  /* in */ int i)

     // PRE:   val and i are assigned
     // POST:  IF 0 <= i < size of this array THEN
     //            arr[i] == val
     //            ELSE error message

{
    if (i < 0 || i >= size)
    {
        cerr << "Store - invalid index : " << i << endl;
        exit(1);
    }

    arr[i] = val;

}
```

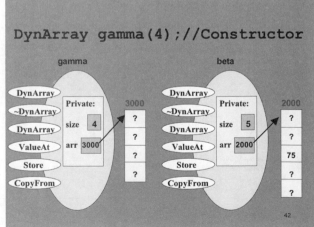

```
DynArray gamma(4);//Constructor
```

Chapter 15

```
gamma.Store(-8,2);
```

```cpp
int  DynArray::ValueAt (/* in */ int i)  const

    // PRE:  i is assigned
    // POST: IF 0 <= i < size THEN
    //          Return value == arr[i]
    //       ELSE halt with error message
{
    if (i < 0 || i >= size)
    {
        cerr << "ValueAt - invalid index : " << i
           << endl;
        exit(1);
    }
    return arr[i];
}
```

## *Why is a destructor needed?*

When a DynArray class variable goes out of
scope, the memory space for data members size
and pointer arr is deallocated

But the dynamic array that arr points to is not
automatically deallocated

A class destructor is used to deallocate the
dynamic memory pointed to by the data member

## class DynArray Destructor

```
DynArray::~DynArray();
   // Destructor
   // POST: Memory for dynamic array deallocated
{
   delete [ ] arr;
}
```

46

## What happens . . .

● *When a function is called that passes a DynArray object by value, what happens?*

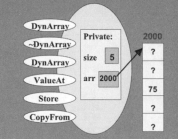

47

## Passing a Class Object by Value

```
// Function code

void  SomeFunc(DynArray  someArr)
   // Uses pass by value
{
       .
       .
       .
       .
}
```

48

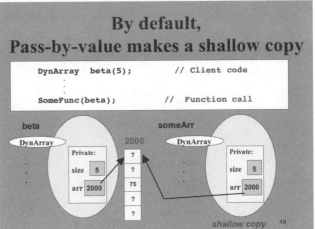

### By default,
### Pass-by-value makes a shallow copy

```
DynArray  beta(5);          // Client code
      .
      .
SomeFunc(beta);             //  Function call
```

*shallow copy*

## Shallow Copy vs. Deep Copy

- *A shallow copy* copies only the class data members, and does not make a copy of any pointed-to data

- *A deep copy* copies not only the class data members, but also makes a separate stored copy of any pointed-to data

## What's the difference?

- *A shallow copy* shares the pointed to dynamic data with the original class object

- *A deep copy* makes its own copy of the pointed to dynamic data at different locations than the original class object

## Making a (Separate) Deep Copy

deep copy

## Initialization of Class Objects

- C++ defines initialization to mean
  - initialization in a variable declaration
  - passing an object argument by value
  - returning an object as the return value of a function

- By default, C++ uses shallow copies for these initializations

## As a result . . .

- When a class has a data member that points to dynamically allocated data, you must write what is called a copy constructor

- The copy constructor is implicitly called in initialization situations and makes a deep copy of the dynamic data in a different memory location

## More about Copy Constructors

- When you provide (write) a copy constructor for a class, the copy constructor is used to make copies for pass by value

- You do not explicitly call the copy constructor

- Like other constructors, it has no return type

- Because the copy constructor properly defines pass by value for your class, it must use pass by reference in its definition

55

## Copy Constructor

- Copy constructor is a special member function of a class that is implicitly called in these 3 situations:

  - Passing object parameters by value

  - Initializing an object variable in its declaration

  - Returning an object as the return value of a function

56

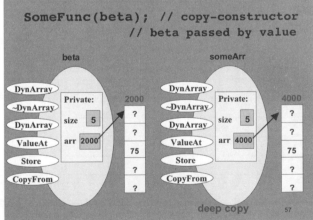

```
SomeFunc(beta);  // copy-constructor
                 // beta passed by value
```

deep copy    57

# Notes

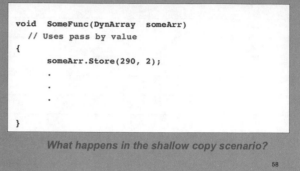

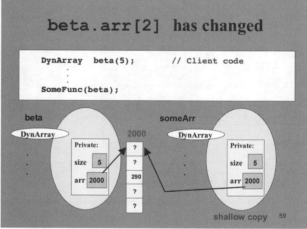

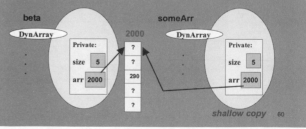

**Classes with Data Member Pointers Need**

CONSTRUCTOR

COPY CONSTRUCTOR

DESTRUCTOR

61

```
DynArray::DynArray(const DynArray& otherArr)
    // Copy constructor
    // Implicitly called for deep copy in initializations
    // POST:  If room on free store THEN
    //    new array of size otherArr.size is created
    //    on free store && arr == its base address
    //    && size == otherArr.size
    //    && arr[0..size-1] == otherArr.arr[0..size-1]
    //    ELSE error occurs
{
    int i;
    size = otherArr.size;
    arr = new  int[size];    // Allocate memory for copy

    for (i = 0; i< size; i++)
        arr[i] = otherArr.arr[i];    // Copies array

}
```
62

## *What about the assignment operator?*

- The default method used for assignment of class objects makes a shallow copy

- If your class has a data member that points to dynamic data, you should write a member function to create a deep copy of the dynamic data

63

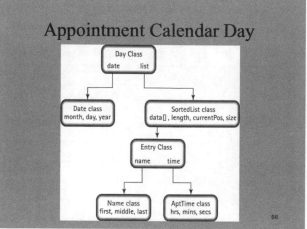

```
gamma.CopyFrom(beta);
```

gamma        beta

DynArray     Private:      3000        DynArray     Private:      2000
~DynArray    size  5        ?          ~DynArray    size  5        ?
DynArray     arr  3000      ?          DynArray     arr  2000      ?
ValueAt                    75          ValueAt                    75
Store                       ?          Store                       ?
CopyFrom                    ?          CopyFrom                    ?

*deep copy*                64

```
void  DynArray::CopyFrom (/* in */ DynArray  otherArr)
      // Creates a deep copy of otherArr
      // POST:  Array pointed to by arr@entry deallocated
      //    &&  IF room on free store
      //        THEN new array is created on free store
      //             && arr == its base address
      //             && size == otherArr.size
      //             && arr[0..size-1] == otherArr[0..size-]
      //        ELSE halts with error message
{
   int i;

   delete[ ]  arr;        // Delete current array
   size = otherArr.size;
   arr = new int [size];          // Allocate new array

   for (i = 0; i< size; i++)  // Deep copy array
       arr[i] = otherArr.arr[i];
}
                                                              65
```

## Appointment Calendar Day

Day Class
date    list

Date class                SortedList class
month, day, year          data[], length, currentPos, size

                          Entry Class
                          name    time

                Name class              AptTime class
                first, middle, last     hrs, mins, secs
                                                          66
```
```

**Notes**

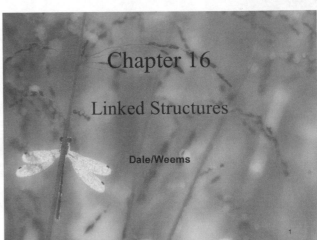

## Chapter 16 Topics

- Meaning of a Linked List
- Meaning of a Dynamic Linked List
- Traversal, Insertion and Deletion of Elements in a Dynamic Linked List
- Specification of a Dynamic Linked Sorted List
- Insertion and Deletion of Elements in a Dynamic Linked Sorted List

## *What is a List?*

- A list is a varying-length, linear collection of homogeneous elements

- Linear means that each list element (except the first) has a unique predecessor and each element (except the last) has a unique successor

## To implement the List ADT

The programmer must

1) choose a concrete data representation for the list, and

2) implement the list operations

4

## Recall:
## 4 Basic Kinds of ADT Operations

- Constructors -- create a new instance (object) of an ADT

- Transformers -- change the state of one or more of the data values of an instance

- Observers -- allow client to observe the state of one or more of the data values of an instance without changing them

- Iterators -- allow client to access the data values in sequence

5

## List Operations

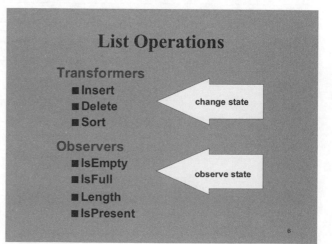

Transformers
- ■ Insert
- ■ Delete          change state
- ■ Sort

Observers
- ■ IsEmpty
- ■ IsFull           observe state
- ■ Length
- ■ IsPresent

6

## ADT List Operations

Iterator
- Reset
- GetNextItem

⟵ Iteration Pair

- Reset prepares for the iteration
- GetNextItem returns the next item in sequence
- No transformer can be called between calls to GetNextItem *(Why?)*

7

## Array-based class List

- SelSort
- IsEmpty
- IsFull
- Length
- Insert
- Delete
- IsPresent
- Reset
- GetNexItem

Private data:
length
data [0]
[1]
[2]

[MAX_LENGTH-1]

currentPos

8

```
// Specification file array-based list ("list.h")
const int MAX_LENGTH = 50;
typedef int   ItemType;

class List              // Declares a class data type
{
public:                 // Public member functions

   List();              // constructor
   bool IsEmpty () const;
   bool IsFull () const;
   int Length ()  const; // Returns length of list
   void Insert (ItemType  item);
   void Delete (ItemType  item);
   bool IsPresent(ItemType  item)  const;
   void SelSort ();
   void Reset ();
   ItemType GetNextItem ();

private:             // Private data members
   int length;    // Number of values currently stored
   ItemType data[MAX_LENGTH];
   int  CurrentPos;  // Used in iteration
};
```
9

## Implementation Structures

- Use a built-in array stored in contiguous memory locations, implementing operations Insert and Delete by moving list items around in the array, as needed
- Use a linked list in which items are not necessarily stored in contiguous memory locations
- A linked list avoids excessive data movement from insertions and deletions

10

## Implementation Possibilities for a List ADT

```
                    List
        ┌─────────────┴─────────────┐
  Built-in array              Linked list
                          ┌────────┴────────┐
                      Built-in         Built-in array
                   dynamic data         of structs
                   and pointers
```

11

## A Linked List

- A linked list is a list in which the order of the components is determined by an explicit link member in each node
- Each node is a `struct` containing a data member and a link member that gives the location of the next node in the list

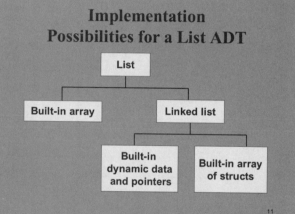

head →  'X' →  'C' →  'L'

12

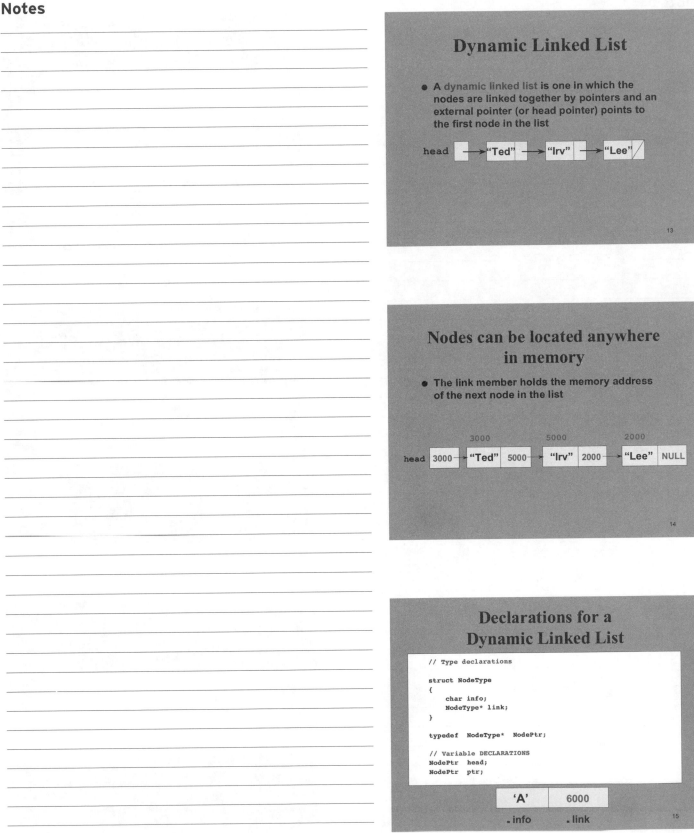

## Dynamic Linked List

● A dynamic linked list is one in which the nodes are linked together by pointers and an external pointer (or head pointer) points to the first node in the list

head ──→ "Ted" ──→ "Irv" ──→ "Lee"

13

## Nodes can be located anywhere in memory

● The link member holds the memory address of the next node in the list

head 3000 ──→ "Ted" 5000 ──→ "Irv" 2000 ──→ "Lee" NULL

14

## Declarations for a Dynamic Linked List

```
// Type declarations

struct NodeType
{
    char info;
    NodeType* link;
}

typedef NodeType* NodePtr;

// Variable DECLARATIONS
NodePtr  head;
NodePtr  ptr;
```

| 'A' | 6000 |
|-----|------|

. info      . link

15

**Notes**

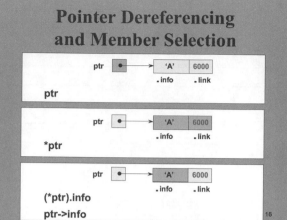

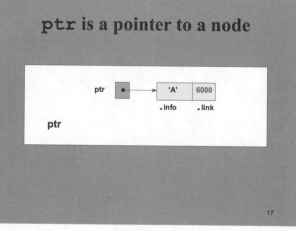

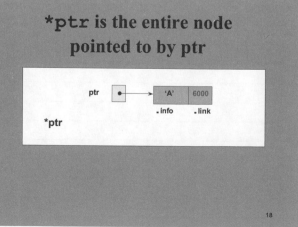

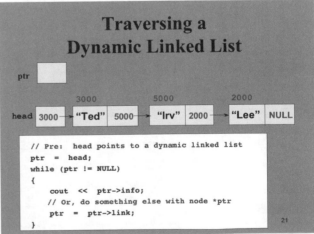

**ptr->info**
**is a node member**

ptr->info

(*ptr).info        // Equivalent

19

**ptr->link**
**is a node member**

ptr->link

(*ptr).link        // Equivalent

20

**Traversing a**
**Dynamic Linked List**

```
// Pre:  head points to a dynamic linked list
ptr = head;
while (ptr != NULL)
{
    cout << ptr->info;
    // Or, do something else with node *ptr
    ptr = ptr->link;
}
```

21

## Notes

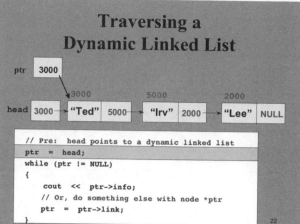

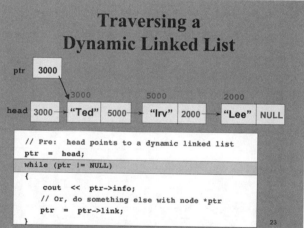

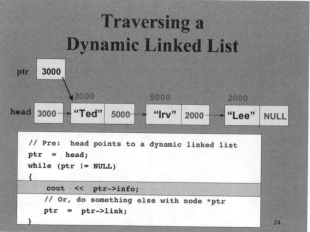

**Notes**

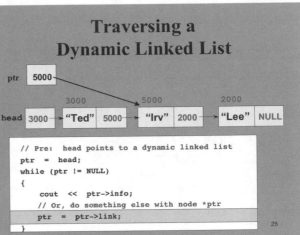

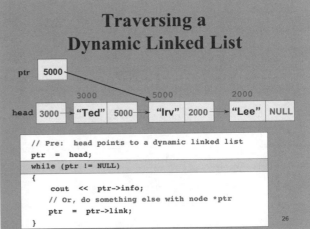

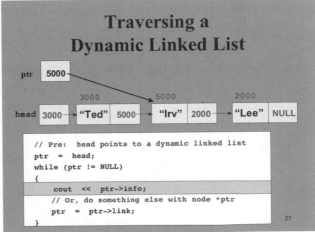

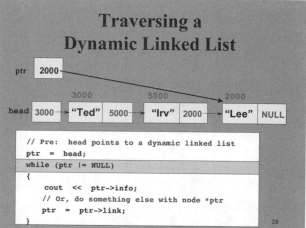

## Traversing a Dynamic Linked List

```
// Pre:  head points to a dynamic linked list
ptr = head;
while (ptr != NULL)
{
    cout << ptr->info;
    // Or, do something else with node *ptr
    ptr = ptr->link;
}
```

## Traversing a Dynamic Linked List

```
// Pre:  head points to a dynamic linked list
ptr = head;
while (ptr != NULL)
{
    cout << ptr->info;
    // Or, do something else with node *ptr
    ptr = ptr->link;
}
```

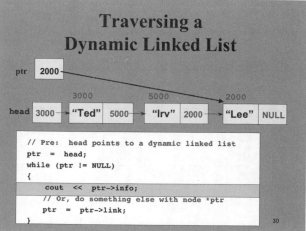

## Traversing a Dynamic Linked List

```
// Pre:  head points to a dynamic linked list
ptr = head;
while (ptr != NULL)
{
    cout << ptr->info;
    // Or, do something else with node *ptr
    ptr = ptr->link;
}
```

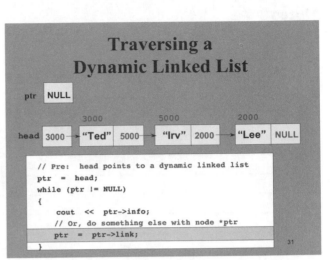

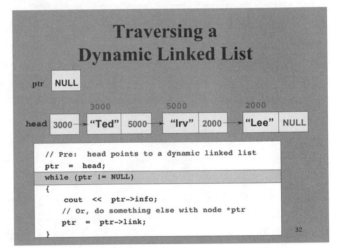

## Using Operator new

Recall

- If memory is available in the free store (or heap), operator new allocates the requested object and returns a pointer to the memory allocated

- The dynamically allocated object exists until the delete operator destroys it

33

Inserting a Node at the Front of a List

```
char      item = 'B';
NodePtr  location;
location = new  NodeType;
location->info = item;
location->link = head;
head = location;
```

Inserting a Node at the Front of a List

```
char      item = 'B';
NodePtr  location;
location = new  NodeType;
location->info = item;
location->link = head;
head = location;
```

Inserting a Node at the Front of a List

```
char      item = 'B';
NodePtr  location;
location = new  NodeType;
location->info = item;
location->link = head;
head = location;
```

# Notes

_____

_____

_____

_____

_____

_____

_____

_____

_____

_____

_____

_____

_____

_____

_____

_____

_____

_____

_____

_____

_____

_____

_____

_____

_____

_____

_____

_____

## Inserting a Node at the Front of a List

item `'B'`

```
char      item = 'B';
NodePtr  location;
location = new  NodeType;
location->info = item;
location->link = head;
head = location;
```

head → 'X' → 'C' → 'L'

location → 'B'

37

## Inserting a Node at the Front of a List

item `'B'`

```
char      item = 'B';
NodePtr  location;
location = new  NodeType;
location->info = item;
location->link = head;
head = location;
```

head → 'X' → 'C' → 'L'

location → 'B'

38

## Inserting a Node at the Front of a List

item `'B'`

```
char      item = 'B';
NodePtr  location;
location = new  NodeType;
location->info = item;
location->link = head;
head = location;
```

head → 'X' → 'C' → 'L'

location → 'B'

39

## Notes

### Using Operator delete

When you use the operator delete
- The object currently pointed to by the pointer is deallocated and the pointer is considered undefined
- The object's memory is returned to the free store

40

### Deleting the First Node from the List

item

```
NodePtr  tempPtr;

item = head->info;
tempPtr = head;
head = head->link;
delete  tempPtr;
```

head  →  'B'  →  'X'  →  'C'  →  'L'

tempPtr

41

### Deleting the First Node from the List

item  'B'

```
NodeType *  tempPtr;

item = head->info;
tempPtr = head;
head = head->link;
delete  tempPtr;
```

head  →  'B'  →  'X'  →  'C'  →  'L'

tempPtr

42

## Notes

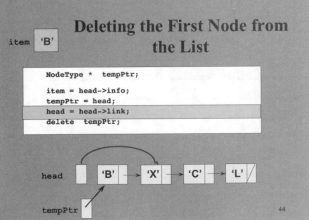

**Deleting the First Node from the List**

item `'B'`

```
NodeType * tempPtr;

item = head->info;
tempPtr = head;
head = head->link;
delete tempPtr;
```

head → 'B' → 'X' → 'C' → 'L'

tempPtr

43

**Deleting the First Node from the List**

item `'B'`

```
NodeType * tempPtr;

item = head->info;
tempPtr = head;
head = head->link;
delete tempPtr;
```

head    'B' → 'X' → 'C' → 'L'

tempPtr

44

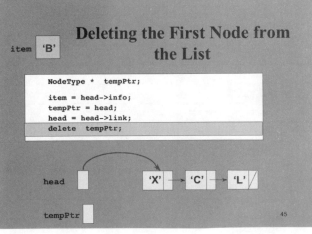

**Deleting the First Node from the List**

item `'B'`

```
NodeType * tempPtr;

item = head->info;
tempPtr = head;
head = head->link;
delete tempPtr;
```

head    'X' → 'C' → 'L'

tempPtr

45

## What is a Sorted List?

A **sorted list** is a variable-length, linear collection of homogeneous elements, ordered according to the value of one or more data members

The transformer operations must maintain the ordering

In addition to Insert and Delete, let's add two new operations to our list

*InsertAsFirst* and *RemoveFirst*

46

## ADT HybridList Operations

Transformers
- InsertAsFirst
- Insert
- RemoveFirst
- Delete

change state

Same observers and iterators as ADT List

Since we have two insertion and two deletion operations, let's call this a Hybrid List

47

## struct NodeType

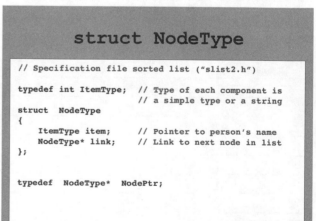

```
// Specification file sorted list ("slist2.h")

typedef int ItemType;    // Type of each component is
                         // a simple type or a string
struct  NodeType
{
    ItemType item;       // Pointer to person's name
    NodeType* link;      // Link to next node in list
};


typedef  NodeType*  NodePtr;
```

48

```
// Specification file  hybrid sorted list("slist2.h")
class  HybridList
{
public:

    bool IsEmpty () const;

    void InsertAsFirst (/* in */  ItemType  item);

    void Insert (/* in */  ItemType  item);

    void RemoveFirst(/* out */  ItemType&  item);

    void Delete (/* in */  ItemType  item);
    void Print () const;
    HybridList ();    // Constructor
    ~HybridList ();   // Destructor
    HybridList (const HybridList&  otherList);
                    // Copy-constructor

private:

    NodeType*  head;
};
```
49

class HybridList

HybridList
~HybridList
IsEmpty
Print
InsertASFirst
Insert
RemoveFirst
Delete

Private data:

head

'C' → 'L' → 'X'

50

# Insert Algorithm

- What will be the algorithm to Insert an item into its proper place in a sorted linked list?

- That is, for a linked list whose elements are maintained in ascending order?

51

## Insert algorithm for HybridList

- Find proper position for the new element in the sorted list using two pointers prevPtr and currPtr, where prevPtr trails behind currPtr

- Obtain a new node and place item in it

- Insert the new node by adjusting pointers

52

## Implementing HybridList Member Function Insert

```
// Dynamic linked list implementation ("slist2.cpp")

void  HybridList::Insert (/* in */  ItemType  item)
// PRE:
//    item is assigned && components in ascending order
// POST:
//    item is in List && components in ascending order
{
          .
          .
          .

}
```

53

## Inserting 'S' into a List

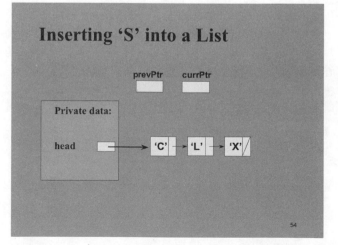

54

# Notes

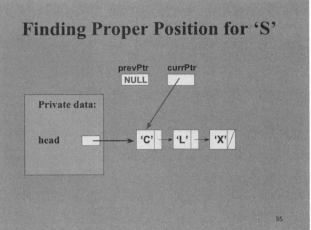

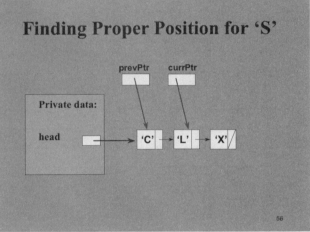

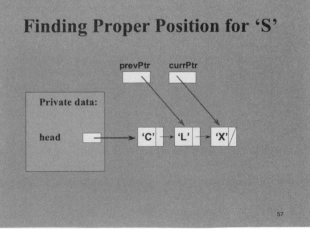

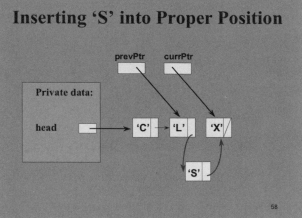

## Inserting 'S' into Proper Position

58

```
// Implementation file for HybridList ("slist.cpp")
HybridList::HybridList ()   // Constructor
// Post: head == NULL
{
    head = NULL;
}


HybridList::~HybridList () // Destructor
// Post: All linked nodes deallocated
{
    ItemType  temp;
    // Keep deleting top node
    while (!IsEmpty)
        RemoveFirst (temp);
}
```
59

```
void  HybridList::Insert(/* in */  ItemType  item)
// Pre: item is assigned && components in ascending order
// Post: new node containing item is in its proper place
//       && components in ascending order
{
    NodePtr currPtr;
    NodePtr prevPtr;
    NodePtr location;
    location = new  NodeType;
    newNodePtr->link = item;
    prevPtr = NULL;
    currPtr = head;
    while (currPtr != NULL  &&   item > currPtr->info )
    {
        prevPtr = currPtr;         // Advance both pointers
        currPtr = currPtr->link;
    }
    location->link = currPtr;// Insert new node here
    if  (prevPtr == NULL)
        head = location;
    else
        prevPtr->link = location;
}
```
60

# Notes

_____
_____
_____
_____
_____
_____
_____
_____
_____
_____
_____
_____
_____
_____
_____
_____
_____
_____
_____
_____
_____
_____
_____
_____
_____
_____
_____
_____
_____
_____
_____
_____
_____
_____
_____
_____
_____
_____

```cpp
void HybridList::InsertAsFirst(/* in */  ItemType  item)
// Pre: item is assigned &&  components in ascending order
// Post: New node containing item is the first item in the list
//     && components in ascending order
{
    NodePtr newNodePtr = new NodeType;

    newNodePtr -> component = item;
    newNodePtr -> link = head;
    head = newNodePtr;
}
Void HybridList::Print() const
// Post: All values within nodes have been printed
{
    NodePtr currPtr = head;  // Loop control pointer
    while (currPtr != NULL)
    {
        cout << currPtr->component << endl;
        currPtr = currPtr->link;
    }
}
```
61

```cpp
void  HybridList::RemoveFirst (
      /* out */  ItemType&  item)
// Pre: list is not empty && components in ascending order
// Post: item == element of first list node @ entry
//    &&  node containing item is no longer in list
//    &&  list components in ascending order
{
    NodePtr  tempPtr = head;
    // Obtain item and advance head
    item = head->info ;
    head = head->link;
    delete  tempPtr;
}
```
62

```cpp
void  HybridList::Delete (/* in */  ItemType  item)
// Pre: list is not empty && components in ascending order
//      && item == component member of some list node
// Post: item == element of first list node @ entry
//       && node containing first occurrence of item no longer
//       in list  && components in ascending order
{
    NodePtr   delPtr;
    NodePtr   currPtr; // Is item in first node?
    if (item == head->info)
    {  // If so, delete first node
        delPtr = head;
        head = head->link;
    }
    else {// Search for item in rest of list
    {
        currPtr = head;
        while (currPtr->link->info  !=  item)
            currPtr = currPtr->link;
        delPtr = currPtr->link;
        currPtr->link = currPtr->link->link;
    }
    delete  delPtr;
}
```
63

## Copy Constructor

Most difficult algorithm so far
  If the original is empty, the copy is
    empty
  Otherwise, make a copy of the head
    with pointer to it
  Loop through original, copying each
    node and adding it to the copy until you
    reach the end
*See Chapter 18 for an easy, elegant solution*

64

## A Month of Day Lists

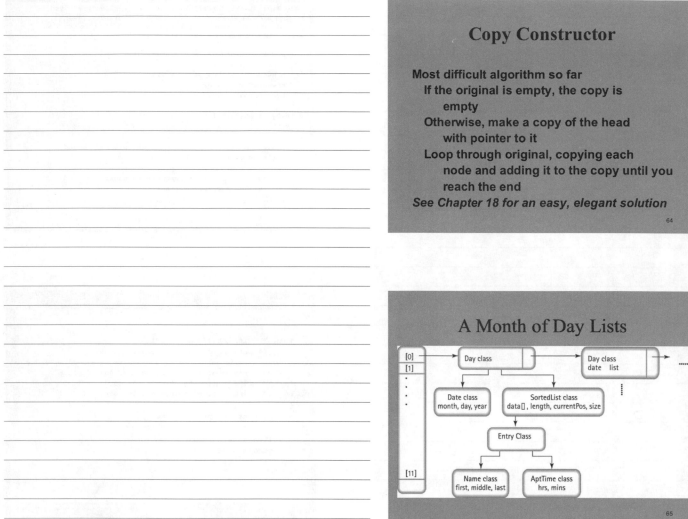

65

## Notes

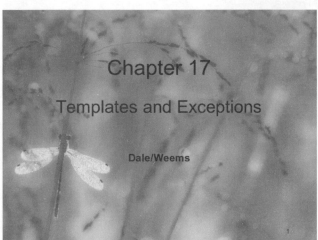

## Chapter 17 Topics

- C++ Function Templates
- Instantiating a Function Templates
- User-defined Specializations
- C++ Class Templates
- Instantiating Class Templates
- Function Definitions for Members of a Template Class
- Exception Classes, Throwing an Exception
- Exception Handlers

## Generic Algorithms

- Generic algorithms are algorithms in which the actions or steps are defined, but the data types of the items being manipulated are not

**Notes**

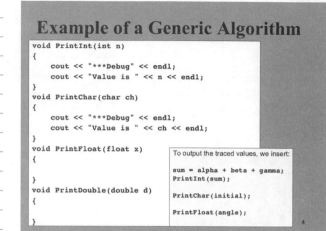

### Example of a Generic Algorithm

```
void PrintInt(int n)
{
    cout << "***Debug" << endl;
    cout << "Value is " << n << endl;
}
void PrintChar(char ch)
{
    cout << "***Debug" << endl;
    cout << "Value is " << ch << endl;
}
void PrintFloat(float x)
{

}
void PrintDouble(double d)
{

}
```

To output the traced values, we insert:
```
sum = alpha + beta + gamma;
PrintInt(sum);

PrintChar(initial);

PrintFloat(angle);
```

4

### Function Overloading

- Function overloading is the use of the same name for different functions, distinguished by their parameter lists

  - Eliminates need to come up with many different names for identical tasks

  - Reduces the chance of unexpected results caused by using the wrong function name

5

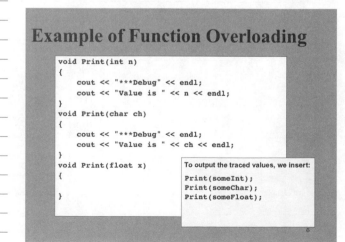

### Example of Function Overloading

```
void Print(int n)
{
    cout << "***Debug" << endl;
    cout << "Value is " << n << endl;
}
void Print(char ch)
{
    cout << "***Debug" << endl;
    cout << "Value is " << ch << endl;
}
void Print(float x)
{

}
```

To output the traced values, we insert:
```
Print(someInt);
Print(someChar);
Print(someFloat);
```

6

## Function Template

• A C++ language construct that allows the compiler to generate multiple versions of a function by allowing parameterized data types

FunctionTemplate

> Template < TemplateParamList >
> FunctionDefinition

TemplateParamDeclaration

> class
>                Identifier
> typename

7

## Example of a Function Template

```
template<class SomeType>          Template
                                  parameter
void Print(SomeType val)
{
    cout << "***Debug" << endl;
    cout << "Value is " << val << endl;
}

        Template              To output the traced values, we insert:
        argument
                              Print<int>(sum);
                              Print<char>(initial);
                              Print<float>(angle);
```

8

## Instantiating a Function Template

• When the compiler instantiates a template, it substitutes the template argument for the template parameter throughout the function template

TemplateFunction Call

> Function < TemplateArgList > (FunctionArgList)

9

## Generic Functions, Function Overloading, Template Functions

| Generic Function | Function Overloading |
|---|---|
| Different Function Definitions | Different Function Definitions |
| Different Function Names | Same Function Name |

**Template Functions**
One Function Definition (a function template)
Compiler Generates Individual Functions

10

## User-Defined Specializations

Example that demonstrates use of `template < >`

```
template<>
void Print(string    vName,    // Name of the variable
           StatusType val )    // Value of the variable
{
    cout << "***Debug" << endl;
    cout << "Value of " << vName << " = ";
    switch (val)
```

11

## Example, continued.

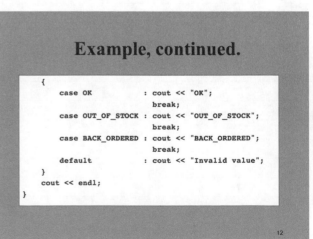

```
    {
        case OK            : cout << "OK";
                             break;
        case OUT_OF_STOCK  : cout << "OUT_OF_STOCK";
                             break;
        case BACK_ORDERED  : cout << "BACK_ORDERED";
                             break;
        default            : cout << "Invalid value";
    }
    cout << endl;
}
```

12

## Organization of Program Code

Three possibilities:

1. Template definitions at the beginning of program file, prior to `main` function

2. Function prototypes first, then the `main` function, then the template definitions

3. Template definition in the header file, use #include to insert that file into the program

13

## What is a Generic Data Type?

- It is a type for which the operations are defined but the data types of the items being manipulated are not

14

## What is a Class Template?

- It is a C++ language construct that allows the compiler to generate multiple versions of a class by allowing parameterized data types

15

## Example of a Class Template

```
template<class ItemType>
class GList
{
public:
    bool IsEmpty() const;
    bool IsFull() const;
    int  Length() const;
    void Insert(/* in */ ItemType item);
    void Delete(/* in */ ItemType item);
    bool IsPresent(/* in */ ItemType item) const;
    void SelSort();
    void Reset() const;
    ItemType GetNextItem();
    GList();                        // Constructor
private:
    int      length;
    ItemType data[MAX_LENGTH];
};
```

Template parameter

16

## Instantiating a Class Template

To create lists of different data types

```
// Client code
                        template argument
GList<int> list1;
GList<float> list2;
GList<string> list3;

list1.Insert(356);
list2.Insert(84.375);
list3.Insert("Muffler bolt");
```

Compiler generates 3 distinct class types

```
GList_int list1;
GList_float list2;
GList_string list3;
```

17

## Instantiating a Class Template

- Class template arguments *must* be explicit
- The compiler generates distinct class types called template classes or generated classes
- When instantiating a template, a compiler substitutes the template argument for the template parameter throughout the class template

18

## Substitution Example

```
class GList_int
{
public:                                    ── int

void Insert(/* in */ (ItemType) item);
                                           ── int
    void Delete(/* in */ (ItemType) item);

    bool IsPresent(/* in */ (ItemType) item) const;
                                           ── int
private:
    int      length;
    (ItemType) data[MAX_LENGTH];
};
         ── int
```

19

## Writing Function Templates

```
template<class ItemType>
void GList<ItemType>::Insert(/* in */ ItemType item)
{
    data[length] = item;
    length++;
}
```

```
void GList<float>::Insert(/* in */ float item)
{
    data[length] = item;
    length++;
}
```

20

## Organization of Program Code

- A compiler must know the argument to the template in order to generate a function template, and this argument is located in the client code
- Solutions
  - Have specification file include implementation file
  - Combine specification file and implementation file into one file

21

## Warning!

*Are you using an IDE (integrated development environment) where the editor, compiler, and linker are bundled into one application?*

Remember **The compiler must know the template argument**

**How you organize the code in a project may differ depending on the IDE you are using**

22

## An Exception is...

An **exception** is an unusual, often unpredictable event, detectable by software or hardware, that requires special processing; also, in C++, a variable or class object that represents an exceptional event

An **exception handler** is a section of program code that is executed when a particular exception occurs

23

## The throw Statement

Throw: to signal the fact that an exception has occurred; also called *raise*

ThrowSt

```
throw Expression
```

24

## The `try-catch` Statement

How one part of the program catches and processes the exception that another part of the program throws.

**TryCatchStatement**

```
try
  Block
catch (FormalParameter)
  Block
catch (FormalParameter)
```

**FormalParameter**

```
{ DataType VariableName
   ...
```

25

## Example of a `try-catch` Statement

```
try
{
    // Statements that process personnel data and may throw
    // exceptions of type int, string, and SalaryError
}
catch (int)
{
    // Statements to handle an int exception
}
```

26

## `try-catch` Continued

```
catch (string s)
{
    cout << s << endl; // Prints "Invalid customer age"
    // More statements to handle an age error
}
catch (SalaryError)
{
    // Statements to handle a salary error
}
```

27

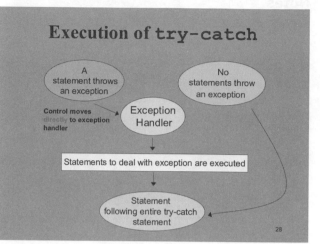

## Execution of try-catch

A statement throws an exception

No statements throw an exception

Control moves directly to exception handler

Exception Handler

Statements to deal with exception are executed

Statement following entire try-catch statement

28

## Selecting an Exception Handler

The computer

• Examines data types of the formal parameters in exception handlers

• Searches in a "north-to-south" order

• Selects first formal parameter whose data type matches that of the thrown exception

• Ellipse parameters are a "wild card" and catch all (*Place the "catch all" handler last*)

29

## More on Selecting Exception Handlers

• The parameter's name is needed only if statements in the body of the exception handler use that variable

• It is a good idea to use only

▪ user-defined classes (and structs) as exception types

▪ one type per exception

▪ descriptive identifiers

30

## Nonlocal Exception Handlers

• It is more common for the throw to occur inside a function that is *called* from within a try-clause than for the throw to be located *within* the try-catch statement

31

## Throwing an Exception to be Caught by the Calling Code

```
void Func3()
{
    try
    {
        Func4();
    }
    catch (ErrType)
    {
    }
}
```

Function call

Normal return

```
void Func4()
{
    if (error)
        throw ErrType();
}
```

Return from thrown exception

32

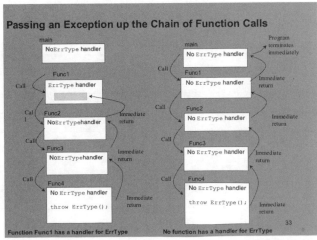

Passing an Exception up the Chain of Function Calls

Function Func1 has a handler for ErrType          No function has a handler for ErrType

33

## Re-Throwing an Exception

- The throw expression is optional
  ```
  throw;
  ```

- Re-throwing an exception in C++ allows
  partial exception handling

34

## Standard Exceptions

- Exceptions Thrown by the Language
  - `new, dynamic_cast, typeid, exception specification`

- Exceptions Thrown by Standard Library Routines
  - Facilities inherited from the C language
  - Facilities designed specifically for C++

35

## Dividing by ZERO

Apply what you know:

```
int Quotient(/* in */ int numer,   // The numerator
             /* in */ int denom)   // The denominator
{
    if (denom != 0)
        return numer / denom;
    else
        // What to do??
}
```

36

## Notes

### A Solution

```
// "quotient.cpp" -- Quotient program

#include<iostream>
#include <string>

using namespace std;

int Quotient(int, int);

class DivByZero   // Exception class
{};

int main()
{
    int numer;   // Numerator
    int denom;   // Denominator
    cout << "Enter numerator and denominator: ";
```
37

```
    cin >> numer >> denom;
    while (cin)
    {
        try
        {
            cout << "Their quotient: "
                 << Quotient(numer, denom) << endl;
        }
        catch (DivByZero)
        {
            cout << "*** Denominator can't be 0"
                 << endl;
        }
        cout << "Enter numerator and denominator: ";
        cin >> numer >> denom;
    }
    return 0;
}
```
38

```
int Quotient(/* in */ int numer,   // The numerator
             /* in */ int denom)   // The denominator
{
    if (denom == 0)
        throw DivByZero();
    return numer / denom;
}
```
39

## Appointment Calendar

- Replace array-based list with linked list to demonstrate that changing implementation doesn't change client code
- Add exceptions to Appointment Calendar Program

40

**Notes**

## Chapter 18 Topics

- Meaning of Recursion
- Base Case and General Case in Recursive Function Definitions
- Writing Recursive Functions with Simple Type Parameters
- Writing Recursive Functions with Array Parameters
- Writing Recursive Functions with Pointer Parameters
- Understanding How Recursion Works

## Recursive Function Call

- A recursive call is a function call in which the called function is the same as the one making the call

- In other words, *recursion occurs when a function calls itself!*

- But we need to avoid making an infinite sequence of function calls (infinite recursion)

## Finding a Recursive Solution

- A recursive solution to a problem must be written carefully

- The idea is for each successive recursive call to bring you one step closer to a situation in which the problem can easily be solved

- This easily solved situation is called the base case

- Each recursive algorithm must have at least one base case, as well as a general (recursive) case

4

## General format for Many Recursive Functions

```
if  (some easily-solved condition)     // Base case

    solution statement

else                                   // General case

    recursive function call
```

Some examples . . .

## Writing a Recursive Function to Find the Sum of the Numbers from 1 to n

DISCUSSION

The function call Summation(4) should have value 10, because that is 1 + 2 + 3 + 4

For an easily-solved situation, the sum of the numbers from 1 to 1 is certainly just 1

So our base case could be along the lines of

```
if  (n == 1)
    return 1;
```

6

## Writing a Recursive Function to Find the Sum of the Numbers from 1 to n

Now for the general case...

The sum of the numbers from 1 to n, that is,
1 + 2 + . . . + n    can be written as

n + the sum of the numbers from 1 to (n - 1),
that is,  n +  1 + 2 + . . . + (n - 1)

or,      n  +   Summation(n - 1)

And notice that the recursive call  Summation(n - 1)
gets us "closer" to the base case of  Summation(1)

7

## Finding the Sum of the Numbers from 1 to n

```
int    Summation (/* in */   int    n)
// Computes the sum of the numbers from 1 to
//  n by adding n to the sum of the numbers
//  from 1 to (n-1)
// Precondition: n is assigned && n > 0
// Postcondition: Return value == sum of
//  numbers from 1 to n
{
    if  (n == 1)     // Base case
        return  1;
    else             // General case
        return (n + Summation (n - 1));
}
```
8

## Summation(4) Trace of Call

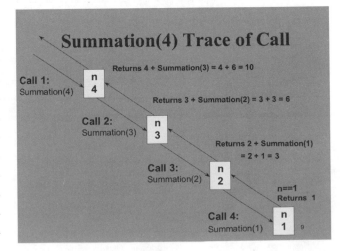

Call 1:
Summation(4)    **n 4**    Returns 4 + Summation(3) = 4 + 6 = 10

Returns 3 + Summation(2) = 3 + 3 = 6

Call 2:
Summation(3)    **n 3**

Returns 2 + Summation(1)
= 2 + 1 = 3

Call 3:
Summation(2)    **n 2**

n==1
Returns 1

Call 4:
Summation(1)    **n 1**    9

## Writing a Recursive Function to Find n Factorial

**DISCUSSION**

The function call Factorial(4) should have value 24, because that is 4 * 3 * 2 * 1

For a situation in which the answer is known, the value of 0! is 1

So our base case could be along the lines of

```
if (number == 0)
    return 1;
```

10

## Writing a Recursive Function to Find Factorial(n)

Now for the general case . . .

The value of Factorial(n) can be written as n * the product of the numbers from (n - 1) to 1, that is,

$$n * (n - 1) * \ldots * 1$$

or, n * Factorial(n - 1)

And notice that the recursive call Factorial(n - 1) gets us "closer" to the base case of Factorial(0)

11

## Recursive Solution

```
int   Factorial ( int   number)
// Pre: number is assigned and number >= 0
{
    if (number == 0)      // Base case
        return 1;
    else                  // General case
        return
        number + Factorial (number - 1);
}
```

12

## Another Example Where Recursion Comes Naturally

- From mathematics, we know that

  $2^0 = 1$ and $2^5 = 2 * 2^4$

- In general,

  $x^0 = 1$ and $x^n = x * x^{n-1}$
  
  for integer x, and integer n > 0

- Here we are defining $x^n$ recursively, in terms of $x^{n-1}$

13

```
// Recursive definition of power function
int  Power ( int   x,    int   n)

// Pre:  n >= 0; x, n are not both zero
// Post: Return value == x raised to the
//   power n.

{
    if  (n == 0)
        return  1; // Base case

    else               // General case
        return ( x * Power (x, n-1))
}
```

Of course, an alternative would have been to use an iterative
solution instead of recursion

14

## Extending the Definition

- *What is the value of $2^{-3}$ ?*
- Again from mathematics, we know that it is

  $2^{-3} = 1 / 2^3 = 1 / 8$

- In general,

  $x^n = 1 / x^{-n}$
  
  for non-zero x, and integer n < 0

- Here we again defining $x^n$ recursively, in terms of $x^{-n}$ when n < 0

15

```
// Recursive definition of power function
float  Power ( /* in */  float   x,
               /* in */   int    n)
// Pre:  x  != 0 && Assigned(n)
// Post: Return value == x raised to the power n

{
    if  (n == 0)        // Base case

        return  1;

    else  if  (n > 0)  // First  general  case

        return ( x * Power (x, n - 1));
    else                 // Second general case

        return ( 1.0 / Power (x, - n));

}
```
16

## The Base Case Can Be "Do Nothing"

```
void     PrintStars (/* in */   int    n)
// Prints n asterisks, one to a line
// Precondition:   n is assigned
// Postcondition:
//    IF n <= 0, n stars have been written
//    ELSE call PrintStarg
{
    if  (n <= 0)  // Base case: do nothing
    else
    {
        cout   <<  '*'  <<  endl;
        PrintStars (n - 1);
    }
}                          // Can rewrite as . . .
```
17

## Recursive Void Function

```
void  PrintStars (/* in */  int   n)
//   Prints n asterisks, one to a line
//   Precondition:  n is assigned
//   Postcondition:
//      IF n > 0, call PrintSars
//      ELSE n stars have been written
{
    if  (n > 0)  // General case
    {
        cout  <<  '*'  <<  endl;
        PrintStars (n - 1);
    }
    // Base case is empty else-clause
}
```
18

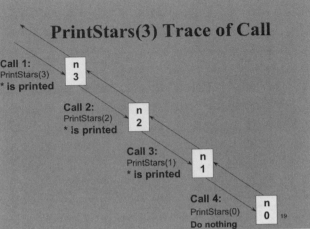

### PrintStars(3) Trace of Call

Call 1:
PrintStars(3)
* is printed

n 3

Call 2:
PrintStars(2)
* is printed

n 2

Call 3:
PrintStars(1)
* is printed

n 1

Call 4:
PrintStars(0)
Do nothing

n 0

19

### Recursive Mystery Function

```
int Find(/* in */ int b, /* in */ int a)
// Simulates a familiar integer operator
// Precondition: a is assigned && a > 0
//    && b is assigned &&    b >= 0
// Postcondition: Return value  ==   ???
{
    if  (b < a)       // Base case
        return  0;
    else              // General case
        return (1 + Find (b - a, a));
}
```
20

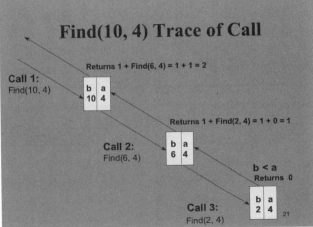

### Find(10, 4) Trace of Call

Returns 1 + Find(6, 4) = 1 + 1 = 2

Call 1:
Find(10, 4)

b 10   a 4

Returns 1 + Find(2, 4) = 1 + 0 = 1

Call 2:
Find(6, 4)

b 6   a 4

b < a
Returns 0

Call 3:
Find(2, 4)

b 2   a 4

21

## Writing a Recursive Function to Print Array Elements in Reverse Order

DISCUSSION

For this task, we will use the prototype:

void PrintRev(const int data[ ], int first, int last);

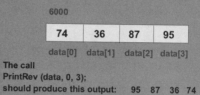

6000

| 74 | 36 | 87 | 95 |
|----|----|----|----|
| data[0] | data[1] | data[2] | data[3] |

The call
PrintRev (data, 0, 3);
should produce this output:    95  87  36  74

22

## Base Case and General Case

A base case may be a solution in terms of a "smaller" array
Certainly for an array with 0 elements, there is no more processing to do

The general case needs to bring us closer to the base case situation
if the length of the array to be processed decreases by 1 with each recursive call, we eventually reach the situation where 0 array elements are left to be processed

In the general case, we could print either the first element, that is, data[first] or we could print the last element, that is, data[last]
Let's print data[last]: After we print data[last], we still need to print the remaining elements in reverse order

23

## Using Recursion with Arrays

```
int PrintRev (
  /* in */ const int data [ ],// Array to be printed
  /* in */        int first,  // Index of first element
  /* in */        int last )  // Index of last element
// Prints items in data [first..last] in reverse order
// Precondition: first assigned  &&  last assigned
//     && if first <= last, data [first..last] assigned
{
    if  (first  <=  last)     // General case
    {
        cout << data[last] << "    "; // Print last
        PrintRev(data, first, last - 1); //Print rest
    }
    // Base case is empty else-clause
}
```
24

## PrintRev(data, 0, 2) Trace

Call 1:
PrintRev(data, 0, 2)
data[2] printed

first 0
last 2

Call 2:
PrintRev(data, 0, 1)
data[1] printed

first 0
last 1

Call 3:
PrintRev(data, 0, 0)
data[0] printed

first 0
last 0

Call 4:
PrintRev(data, 0, -1)
Do nothing

first 0
last -1

NOTE: data address 6000 is also passed

25

## *Why use recursion?*

• These examples could all have been written more easily using iteration

• However, for certain problems the recursive solution is the most natural solution

• This often occurs when structured variables are used

Remember The iterative solution uses a loop, and the recursive solution uses a selection statement

26

## Recursion with Linked Lists

• For certain problems the recursive solution is the most natural solution

• This often occurs when pointer variables are used

27

## struct NodeType

```
typedef  char  ComponentType;

struct  NodeType
{
    ComponentType   component;
    NodeType*       link;
}

NodeType*  head;
```

28

## RevPrint(head);

head

'A' → 'B' • → 'C' → 'D' • → 'E'

FIRST, print out this section of list, backwards

THEN, print
this element

29

## Base Case and General Case

A base case may be a solution in terms of a "smaller" list
Certainly for a list with 0 elements, there is no more
processing to do

Our general case needs to bring us closer to the base case
situation
If the number of list elements to be processed decreases by
1 with each recursive call, the smaller remaining list will
eventually reach the situation where 0 list elements are left
to be processed

In the general case, we print the elements of the (smaller)
remaining list in reverse order and then print the current
element

30

## Using Recursion with a Linked List

```
void  RevPrint (NodeType*   head)

// Pre:  head points to an element of a list
// Post: All elements of list pointed to by head have
//    been printed in reverse order.
{
    if (head != NULL)                // General case
    {
        RevPrint (head-> link); // Process the rest
        // Print currrent
        cout << head->component << endl;
    }
    // Base case : if the list is empty, do nothing
}
```
31

## Recall that . . .

- Recursion occurs when a function calls itself (directly or indirectly)

- Recursion can be used in place of iteration (looping)

- Some functions can be written more easily using recursion

32

## Recursion or Iteration?

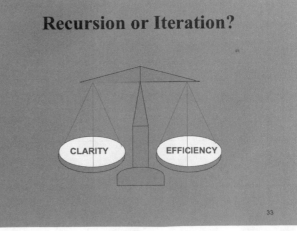

CLARITY    EFFICIENCY

33

### What is the value of Rose (25)?

```
int   Rose (int   n)
{
    if   (n == 1)   // Base case
        return  0;
    else                // General case
        return (1 + Rose(n / 2));
}
```

34

### Finding the Value of Rose (25)

```
  Rose(25)                    the original call
= 1 + Rose(12)                first recursive call
= 1 + (1 + Rose(6))           second recursive call
= 1 + (1 + (1 + Rose(3)))     third recursive call
= 1 + (1 + (1 + (1 + Rose(1)))) fourth recursive call
= 1 +  1 +  1  + 1 + 0
= 4
```

35

### Writing Recursive Functions

- There must be at least one base case and at least one general (recursive) case--the general case should bring you "closer" to the base case

- The arguments(s) in the recursive call cannot all be the same as the formal parameters in the heading, otherwise, infinite recursion would occur

- In function Rose(), the base case occurred when (n == 1) was true--the general case brought us a step closer to the base case, because in the general case the call was to Rose(n/2), and the argument n/2 was closer to 1 (than n was)

36

## When a function is called...

- A transfer of control occurs from the calling block to the code of the function
- It is necessary that there be a return to the correct place in the calling block after the function code is executed
- This correct place is called the return address
- When any function is called, the run-time stack is used--activation record for the function call is placed on the stack

37

## Stack Activation Record

- The activation record (stack frame) contains the return address for this function call, the parameters, local variables, and space for the function's return value (if non-void)

- The activation record for a particular function call is popped off the run-time stack when the final closing brace in the function code is reached, or when a return statement is reached in the function code

- At this time the function's return value, if non-void, is brought back to the calling block return address for use there

38

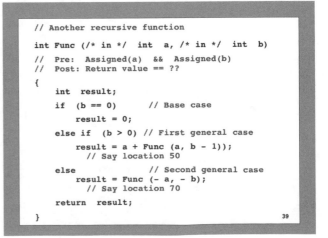

```
// Another recursive function

int Func (/* in */  int  a, /* in */  int  b)
//   Pre:  Assigned(a)  &&  Assigned(b)
//   Post: Return value == ??
{
    int  result;
    if  (b == 0)        // Base case
        result = 0;
    else if  (b > 0) // First general case
        result = a + Func (a, b - 1));
           // Say location 50
    else                // Second general case
        result = Func (- a, - b);
           // Say location 70
    return  result;
}
```

39

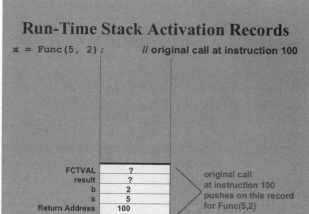

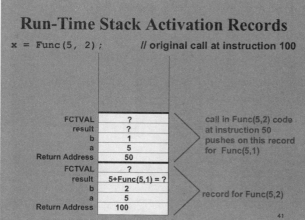

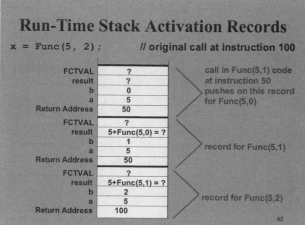

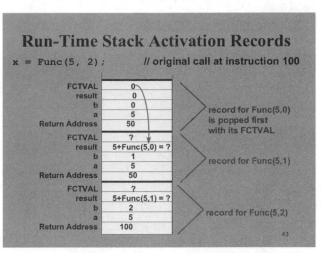

### Run-Time Stack Activation Records

x = Func(5, 2);          // original call at instruction 100

| | |
|---|---|
| FCTVAL | 0 |
| result | 0 |
| b | 0 |
| a | 5 |
| Return Address | 50 |

record for Func(5,0) is popped first with its FCTVAL

| | |
|---|---|
| FCTVAL | ? |
| result | 5+Func(5,0) = ? |
| b | 1 |
| a | 5 |
| Return Address | 50 |

record for Func(5,1)

| | |
|---|---|
| FCTVAL | ? |
| result | 5+Func(5,1) = ? |
| b | 2 |
| a | 5 |
| Return Address | 100 |

record for Func(5,2)

43

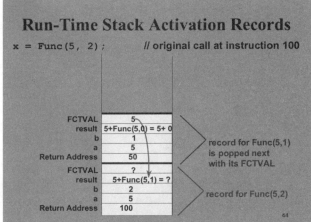

### Run-Time Stack Activation Records

x = Func(5, 2);          // original call at instruction 100

| | |
|---|---|
| FCTVAL | 5 |
| result | 5+Func(5,0) = 5+ 0 |
| b | 1 |
| a | 5 |
| Return Address | 50 |

record for Func(5,1) is popped next with its FCTVAL

| | |
|---|---|
| FCTVAL | ? |
| result | 5+Func(5,1) = ? |
| b | 2 |
| a | 5 |
| Return Address | 100 |

record for Func(5,2)

44

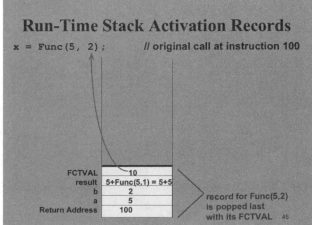

### Run-Time Stack Activation Records

x = Func(5, 2);          // original call at instruction 100

| | |
|---|---|
| FCTVAL | 10 |
| result | 5+Func(5,1) = 5+5 |
| b | 2 |
| a | 5 |
| Return Address | 100 |

record for Func(5,2) is popped last with its FCTVAL   45

## Show Activation Records for these calls

x = Func(- 5, - 3);

x = Func(5, - 3);

*What operation does Func(a, b) simulate?*

46

## Write a function . . .

- Write a function that takes an array a and two subscripts, low and high as arguments, and returns the sum of the elements
  a[low]+..+ a[high]

- Write the function two ways -- one using iteration and one using recursion

- For your recursive definition's base case, for what kind of array do you know the value of Sum(a, low, high) right away?

47

```
// Recursive definition

int  Sum ( /* in */  const  int  a[ ],
           /* in */    int   low,
           /* in */    int   high)
// Pre:  Assigned(a[low..high]) && low <= high
// Post: Return value == sum of items a[low..high]
{
    if  (low == high) // Base case

        return  a [low];

    else                  // General case

        return  a [low] + Sum(a, low + 1, high);

}
```

48

## Notes

_____

_____

_____

_____

_____

_____

_____

_____

_____

_____

_____

_____

_____

_____

_____

_____

_____

_____

_____

_____

_____

_____

_____

_____

_____

_____

_____

_____

_____

_____

_____

_____

```
// Iterative definition

int  Sum ( /* in */  const  int  a[ ],
              /* in */   int   high)
// Pre:  Assigned(a[0..high])
// Post: Return value == sum of items a[0..high]
{
    int sum = 0;
    for (int index= 0; index <= high; index++)

        sum = sum + a[index];
    return sum;

}
```

49

## Write a function . . .

- Write a LinearSearch that takes an array a and two subscripts, low and high, and a key as arguments R
- It returns true if key is found in the elements a[low...high]; otherwise, it returns false

- Write the function two ways - - using iteration and using recursion

- For your recursive definition's base case(s), for what kinds of arrays do you know the value of LinearSearch(a, low, high, key) right away?

50

```
// Recursive definition

bool LinearSearch
    (/* in */ const int a[ ],
     /* in */   int   low,
     /* in */   int   high,
     /* in */   int   key)
// Pre: Assigned(a[low..high])
// Post: IF (key in a[low..high])
//          Return value is true,
//       else return value is false
{
    if  (a [ low ] == key) // Base case

        return true;

    else if (low == high) // Second base case

        return  false;

    else                      // General case

        return
          LinearSearch(a, low + 1, high, key);
}
```

51

Recursion

335

## Iterative Solution

See Chapter 13...

52

## Function BinarySearch()

- BinarySearch that takes sorted array a, and two subscripts, low and high, and a key as arguments
- It returns true if key is found in the elements a[low...high], otherwise, it returns false
- BinarySearch can also be written using iteration or recursion, but it is an inherently recursive algorithm

53

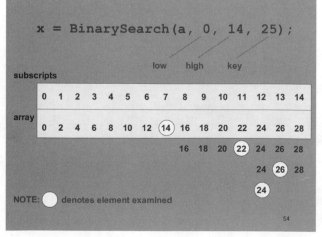

54

## Notes

```
// Recursive definition
bool BinarySearch (/* in */ const int  a[ ],
                   /* in */ int   low,
                   /* in */ int   high,
                   /* in */ int   key)
// Pre:  a[low .. high] in ascending order && Assigned (key)
// Post: IF (key in a[low . . high]), return value is true
//    otherwise return value is false
{
    int  mid;
    if   (low > high)
         return false;
    else
    {
        mid = (low + high) / 2;
        if (a [ mid ] == key)
           return  true;
        else if (key < a[mid]) // Look in lower half
             return BinarySearch(a, low, mid-1, key);
        else  // Look in upper half
             return BinarySearch(a, mid+1, high, key);
    }
}                                                    55
```